I Believe But I Have Questions

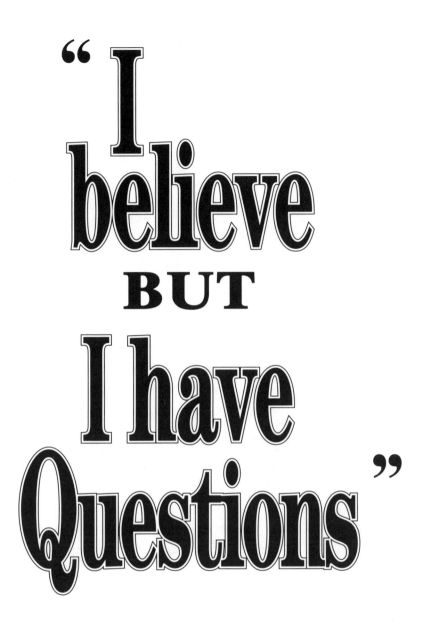

"I believe BUT I have Questions"

Jane L. Fryar

CPH™
SAINT LOUIS

For Kristin

May you know Christ and continue to grow in Him!

Cover photography by Michael Powers

Unless otherwise indicated, Scripture quotations are taken from the HOLY BIBLE, NEW INTERNATIONAL VERSION®. Copyright © 1973, 1978, 1984 by the International Bible Society. Used by permission of Zondervan Publishing House. All rights reserved.

The "NIV" and "New International Version" trademarks are registered in the United States Patent and Trademark Office by the International Bible Society. Use of either trademark requires the permission of the International Bible Society.

Scripture quotations marked NKJV are from New King James edition, copyright © 1979, 1980, 1982. Used by permission.

Scripture quotations marked NASB are from the NEW AMERICAN STANDARD BIBLE, © The Lockman Foundation 1960, 1962, 1963, 1968, 1971, 1972, 1973, 1975, 1977, and are used by permission.

Scripture quotations marked NET are taken from the *HOLY BIBLE: New Testament—New Evangelical Translation*. Copyright © 1992 God's Word to the Nations Bible Society. Used by permission.

Copyright © 1994 Concordia Publishing House
3558 S. Jefferson Avenue, St. Louis, MO 63118-3968
Manufactured in the United States of America

Library of Congress Cataloging-in-Publication Data

Fryar, Jane, 1950–
    Answers to questions new Christians ask / Jane L. Fryar.
      p. cm.
    ISBN 0-570-04636-X:
    1. Christian life—1960– —Miscellanea. 2. Spiritual life—Christianity—Miscellanea. 3. Christian life—Lutheran authors—Miscellanea. I. Title.
BV4501.2.F8 1993
248.4—dc20   93-50560

1 2 3 4 5 6 7 8 9 10   03 02 01 00 99 98 97 96 95 94

Contents

As You Begin . . .

Stuck. That's how I felt a decade or so ago every time I thought about my walk with the Lord. Why did I continue to worry even after I had memorized so many Bible passages assuring me of God's care and protection? Why did I gossip with such predictable regularity even after I had heard so many sermons and read so many books about God's will for the content of my conversation? Why, oh why, was there so little love for others in my life?

I found myself frustrated, exasperated with myself—and with my Lord, too, truth be told. Would I ever change? Whenever I asked that question, a resounding NO echoed down the corridors of my mind.

My friends assured me of God's forgiveness and of His love for me in Jesus despite my sin. And they advised me to trust that God would help me follow Christ more closely.

I treasured the forgiveness. But I didn't understand the advice to "rely on God's power" at all. It sounded, frankly, like so much churchy mumbo jumbo.

So, following Satan's siren song toward the reef of self-improvement (accent on the *self*), I began to look for techniques that would enable me to produce more of the fruit of the Holy Spirit—love, joy, peace, patience, kindness, and all the rest—in my own life. In short, I tried. Hard. And I fell. Hard. I tried again. I fell again. Harder.

Again and again I smashed into the rocks of defeat. Sometimes I would succeed in outward obedience to this or that one of God's commands. But then I would find the current of my own effort slamming me against the cliffs of spiritual arrogance. I would look down on others around me, smugly confident that if they would only try harder, they too could succeed. Sooner or later I would recognize the sinful pride in that attitude and careen again into despair.

Misery. It's the only apt descriptor of those years.

But God is merciful. He sent people to me. He opened the Scriptures to my heart. He began to teach me, little by little, what He wants all His children to know and to do about their personal un-Christlikeness. He began to show me what it means to live a grace-based lifestyle. And He continues to help me day by day to grow up in the new life He's given me.

I'm still at times frustrated with the snail-like pace of the process, but I have seen perceptible growth. The genuine kind of growth that honors God because He's the one who has brought it about.

Some Christians seem to take offense at the idea that we can grow in our faith-walk, in what the theologians call sanctification. They see conversation about spiritual growth as an open invitation for believers to compare themselves with one another and to find in that comparison the illegitimate pleasures of spiritual pride.

The apostle Paul recognized those dangers, too. He wrote about that temptation: "We do not dare to classify or compare ourselves with some who commend themselves. When they measure themselves by themselves and compare themselves with themselves, they are not wise" (2 Corinthians 10:12).

Even so, the Holy Spirit also urges us:

"Therefore let us leave the elementary teachings about Christ and go on to maturity" (Hebrews 6:1).

"Like newborn babies, crave pure spiritual milk, so that by it you may grow up in your salvation, now that you have tasted that the Lord is good" (1 Peter 2:2–3).

"But grow in the grace and knowledge of our Lord and Savior Jesus Christ" (2 Peter 3:18).

We must never minimize the dangers of spiritual pride. Yet we must not ignore the dangers of living in spiritual immaturity either.

This book explores the process of spiritual growth and ways to apply the Christian faith in everyday life. First, it emphasizes the truth that we can be sure of God's love, of His forgiveness, and of the eternal life we have in Jesus. These facts are foundational. Until a believer is convinced of them, further growth will be minimal. The chapters that follow talk about growing up in the ability to live Christlike lives as a result of knowing the love of Christ.

As I've written, I've seen ever more clearly how miraculous is the continuing work of the Lord Jesus in my own heart and life. I've appreciated ever more fully the freedom our Lord has given us to walk away each day from what Saint Paul called "the curse of the law" (Galatians 3:13).

Now, as I write this introduction—a task I've saved for last—I pray that the Lord Jesus will use my poor words and through them speak His powerful Word to your heart. I pray that He will cultivate the soil of your heart as only He can, so you will grow as never before in your relationship with Him and in your relationships with your brothers and sisters in the faith, too.

A note about organization. The first four chapters form a foundation for the rest of the book. With a firmness only a former fourth-grade teacher can muster, I suggest that you read these chapters first. After that, feel free to flip ahead to any chapter that catches your eye.

Each chapter begins with a letter from "Lynn" to "Terry." These letters each pose a question or introduce the topic that chapter will address. They also form a kind of spiritual journal, chronicling Lynn's journey of faith during the first year or so of Lynn's walk with the Lord. As you read, it will become apparent that the Holy Spirit used Terry's witness to lead Lynn to faith. Even though Terry moved away shortly afterward, Lynn had come to love and respect Terry as a spiritual mentor—albeit a long-distance one.

If these letters help you define specific questions as you approach each chapter's theme, great! But if you don't find the letters all that helpful, feel free to skip them. You can readily use the book without reading them at all.

May the Lord Jesus draw you ever closer to Himself in love as you read, as you think, and as you continue to grow up to maturity—in Him.

Dear Terry,

Wow! Do I ever miss you and your family. I suppose that doesn't make much sense, since we knew each other such a short time. But as I watched your car pull out of the driveway behind the moving van, my heart sank into the heels of my Reeboks. I know what a great opportunity this new job represents for you and your family, but I hate the fact that it takes you halfway across the continent.

Can it really have been less than a month since you and the others from the church sat on my sofa and talked with me about Jesus? If it hadn't been for that rainstorm, I'm not sure I would have invited the three of you in. You know, after you all left, I cried. Even now I find tears coming to my eyes sometimes.

I've never cried from happiness before. It's a little embarrassing. I sometimes find myself laughing and crying all at once. I feel so . . . well . . . lighthearted.

That word sounds old-fashioned, I suppose. Maybe because not too many people experience the feeling it anymore. I know I never had until you introduced me to my Savior. My heart gave up its burdens. I guess I didn't know I had been carrying so many.

I said something like that to Lisa McClellen this morning in church. She smiled and thanked me for reminding her. She said she always finds it refreshing to spend time with baby Christians. I'm glad I encouraged her, but . . . well . . . can you tell me what she meant?

I guess I qualify as a "baby believer." On the other hand, I feel kind of awkward—a 27-year-old baby? Still, if this lightheartedness and peace are permanent, bring on the strained prunes and teething biscuits!

Thanks, Terry!

In Jesus,

Lynn

[Jesus said,] "You must be born again." John 3:7

Baby? Who's a Baby?

A scream ripped through the black velvet sky above the clearing in the forest. Then another. And another still. Those who heard the shrieks shuddered. They clenched their teeth and their fists as if to harden themselves to the pain. As the screams continued, the listeners steeled themselves to a cold truth—they could do nothing to help.

Nor could the sufferer's husband. He knelt at her side, his arms and legs nearly numb from fear, forced to listen—simply listen—to her cries and to her fierce, irregular breathing. He reached down to clasp her hand. Her nails bit into his flesh.

The contractions washed over her, one after another, so close now as to engulf both John and his wife in one continuous sea of agony. Still the baby would not come. Somehow it had turned itself inside her belly. And now its struggle threatened to strangle the life from both baby and mother.

As the waves of pain rolled on and on, the Moor slipped through the doorway of the rough lean-to. He brushed his hand across the woman's brow as he murmured a word of comfort. Then he faced her husband. The stranger's left hand held a razor-sharp blade. His eyes asked the permission he needed.

Wrenching himself away, John staggered out into the damp night air. He braced himself against a tree awaiting the next set of screams, the ones that were sure to come—the sharpest ones of all. Slowly, ever so slowly, Orion trekked across the cold sky. The screams grew still. Silence roared through the clearing.

Then, a tiny wail. John lunged back into the crude shelter and gathered the still-wet baby into his burly arms. His wife smiled at husband and infant through tired eyes. John smiled back, his eyes damp with the knowledge that she would live. He held the infant in one massive hand as he wound a coarse blanket around it. Then he burst back outside. Holding the infant shoulder-high, he spun in glee through the camp shouting, "My son! My son!"

Movie-makers seldom conjure up more magic than that created by director Kevin Reynolds in this scene from *Robin Hood: Prince of Thieves*. The evening ends with Robin, Maid Marian, and all the fugitives who have found refuge in Sherwood Forest joining hands to celebrate the birth of Little John's infant. They dance the night away, their songs flitting like fairies from leaf to leaf through the woods.

From the beginning of human history, families have celebrated birth. We dance. We sing. We give one another pink and blue bubble-gum cigars. Take a newborn baby into a room and most often a sweet joy brings calm to everyone present. Even pessimists crusty enough to snort bah, humbug at Christmas often find a smile tickling the corners of their lips when they hold a baby.

Bibs. Bottles. Baby powder. Sleepers with feet. Booties and rattles. A first smile. A first tooth. A first step. A first word. In our imagination we paint a baby's world pastel and peaceful.

As any parent knows, though, babies sometimes get colicky. They dirty their diapers. They throw up. Their internal clock gets knocked off kilter and they sleep all day, crying for attention all night.

"You're such a baby!" It's the ultimate insult a disgusted six-year-old can aim and fire at a playmate.

Against the backdrop of joy, wonder, and celebration; against the backdrop of trauma, pain, and tears; against all the experiences we've had with babies, we hear our Lord Jesus say, "You must be born again" (John 3:7) as He calls us to faith and invites us, through Baptism, to die and rise with Him (Romans 6:3–4). We read the words of Peter, one of Jesus' followers, "As newborn babes, desire the pure milk of the word, that you may grow" (1 Peter 2:2 NKJV).

We hear. We read. We wonder. What does it mean to be a baby Christian? Am I one? How do I know? If I am, does that mean there's something wrong with me?

A popular comedian begins his routine, "I started out in life as a baby." All believers start out in their spiritual lives that way too—as baby Christians. There's absolutely nothing wrong with that! It's just what we'd expect.

No one pops out of mom's womb into the world ready to take a drivers' license exam or leave home for Marine Corps boot camp. Just so, newly born Christians do not come into God's family with a deep prayer life or the qualifications to be a Sunday school teacher. There's nothing wrong with that. How could we expect anything else?

Spiritual newborns belong to God's family just as surely as the strongest, most mature soldier of the cross. The heavenly Father opens His heart and stretches out His arms in acceptance and love to both alike. New believers do not join some kind of spiritual underclass in the church of Jesus Christ. You belong! You belong just as much right now as you will when you walk up to the front door of your Father's mansion and find your Savior and His holy angels waiting there to welcome you home.

Newborns must mature. Physical newborns must grow up physically. Spiritual newborns must grow up spiritually. In both cases, God gives the growth. In both cases, growth is a process, not a destination.

So, if you're a newborn in God's family, relax. Celebrate your new birth! Enjoy your new life! Laugh. Dance. Cry with joy. Sing. Bask in the love your Father has for you. Shout your delight. Share your ecstasy with your new brothers and sisters. Watch them smile as they realize again how good it feels to know the freedom of forgiveness and of God's no-strings-attached love for each one of us.

Each chapter in this book will conclude with several questions Christians sometimes ask as they think about that chapter's topic. A brief answer follows each question. If you would like to read more about a given issue, you may want to consult the Bible passages listed at the end of the chapter.

What does it mean to be born again?

Think back to Lynn and what God has done in Lynn's life. Our Lord has given Lynn a brand-new relationship with Himself. He has made Lynn a member of His family. He has forgiven all of Lynn's sins; heaven's hall of records has no file folder containing a list of all the ways Lynn has broken God's Law. No judge on earth would invite a convicted criminal to join his family. Yet that's what our Lord has done for each of us. We receive from heaven's court what we do not deserve—a full pardon and, in addition, a new life.

How does the new birth Jesus talked about happen? How do we get this full pardon and a new life?

God opens His arms and invites us to fall back in His love. He shows us our need—our deep, deep need—for His forgiveness, and then He points us to the cross where Jesus, His Son, bled in agony in our place. Recognizing the emptiness of our hearts, we must give up the hope of winning anything at the bargaining table. When we stop negotiating, when we give up on our own goodness, we find a God who loves us despite our sin. We find a God of passionate love whose Word and whose Son fill our empty hearts and hands with a treasure so big we will never be able to take it all in.

What happens when we're born again, born spiritually?

Something very real. When the Bible talks about the new birth, those words are not just pious double-talk. God plants a seed in our hearts—the seed of new life. That life makes a real difference. God gives us a life with Himself, a relationship with Himself. He gives us a life that makes sense, a life that has meaning and purpose. This life, begun now, will never end. Not even death can steal or spoil what God has done for us. And there's more.

The seed of new life God has planted within us will grow. Those who receive the new birth also are given the potential to become more and more and more like Jesus. We'll never be more fully members of God's family than we are on the day we're reborn. But as God's new life matures in us, people around us will begin to see that little by little we're more like our Father, little by little more like our Brother, Jesus, every day.

What is it like to grow up spiritually?

Just as an infant can't imagine the joy of growing up, new believers can't fully grasp the joy of growing up spiritually either. But if you're born again, God has planted tremendous potential inside you. He takes a very personal interest in nurturing it along. He's the one, the only one, who can bring it to maturity. And He has promised to do that. The longer you live with your Savior, the more you'll realize what an adventure your new life can be.

For further reading: John 3; Philippians 1:1–11

14

Dear Terry,

It was great to hear from you last week. Your encouragement made me feel more comfortable with considering myself a "baby Christian." You're right. What else could anyone expect?

As I've thought it through, though, I've been wondering about the comparison between physical and spiritual birth. If it holds true, then baby Christians must experience some growing up years. My own elementary school and junior high days haven't receded that far into the past! If growing up spiritually is like that, I'll bet I'm in for a real roller-coaster ride!

What will growing up spiritually be like? I mean, do new-born Christians become spiritual children and then (horrors!) spiritual adolescents?

I guess I'm asking what I can expect over, say, the next few months or maybe even years. Will it take that long—years, I mean? And what will it be like when I've reached spiritual maturity?

Thanks again for taking time to think through this with me. You can't know how much it means to me—or, then again, maybe you can!

In Jesus,

Lynn

What Now? What Can I Expect?

Imagine biting into a lemon slice. Savor the tart fragrance. Feel your taste buds burst to life. Your lips begin to pucker—even before your lips close around the fruit. Then feel your teeth tingle as they bite into the bright yellow pulp.

Now imagine explaining this experience to someone who has never seen—much less tasted—a lemon before.

Explaining life in Jesus Christ to someone who has not yet experienced it presents a similar problem. The tingle. The fragrance. The anticipation. And, to be sure, the tartness that Jesus' brothers and sisters sometimes experience in their relationship with Him. These defy description.

Those newly born into God's family find themselves nourished and comforted in the Father's special care. It's as though our Lord enfolds us in a protective bubble. We experience a joy and an optimism we never thought possible before. We're different. We belong to God and to His people. And we know it.

As any good parent understands though, children won't mature in a hot-house environment. Babies need to explore the world around them and experiment with how it works. Babies need to learn lessons of trust. Babies need to stretch and kick and sit up on their own. They need to flex their muscles and learn to coordinate their movements. Babies denied these things fail to thrive. They will never live up to their potential.

That's true spiritually, too, and God knows it. So, after a while, the bubble of euphoria that surrounds us as baby Christians begins to dissolve. The delight we felt during the first months of our new life begins to fade away. It doesn't mean that we're losing our faith. Nor does it mean our Father loves us any less. Remember—His attitude toward us never, ever changes. The universe could blow itself to bits, but when the cosmic dust settled, the Father's love for each one of His children would still stand, rock solid amidst the debris. He has promised:

> "Though the mountains be shaken and the hills be removed,
> yet My unfailing love for you will not be shaken nor My covenant

of peace be removed," says the Lord, who has compassion on you (Isaiah 54:10).

God's love won't change. But sooner or later our feelings will. Listen to what a wise pastor of another generation had to say about that:

> It is the general experience that when a person has become a Christian he soon has pleasant feelings. God deals with His spiritual infants the way an earthly father deals with his little ones. He gives them baby food and sweets. So God at the beginning gives His Christians the sweets of pleasant feelings. But when they have had much experience and have exercised their faith, God takes the sweets away and offers them black bread, which is often quite hard and heavy. God reasons, "You have had sufficient experience in your Christianity, and so this will not tax you too severely. If I would give this bread to the little ones, they would be unable to digest it." In trials Christians often reminisce: "Oh, what a blessed person I once was! How I reveled in sweet feelings, in the joyful certainty that I have a gracious God in heaven." . . .
>
> What a loving Father God is to His Christians! He does not at once lay heavy burdens upon them. He puts them through a training period and only gradually withdraws feelings of comfort, so that they may learn to cling to God in the dark. Hence no one should think that a reduction in pleasant sensations indicates a fall from grace or that one no longer has the first love. The love of a mature, experienced Christian for his Savior may not taste quite as sweet, but it is far purer, because many impurities have been burned off (C. F. W. Walther, Law and Gospel, trans. Herbert J. A. Bouman [St. Louis: Concordia, 1981], pp. 107–8).

Somewhere, then, along the road to spiritual maturity, young Christians become spiritual adolescents. We come to know our Father in a different, deeper way than we did during spiritual infancy. We wrestle with issues of identity and of our place in God's family. We learn to use the gifts and abilities God has given us for the benefit of others in His family. We struggle to find a healthy balance between dependence and independence in our relationship with other believers. We practice the skills we need to confront Satan and his temptations—and win. We grow in our understanding of the Scriptures, and we cultivate the ability to apply God's truths to our everyday lives.

Few human beings glide across the treacherous ice of adolescence with the grace of an Olympic figure skater. Mark Twain is supposed to have given this formula to the parents of teens: When a young person turns 13, pack him into a large pickle barrel and nail the lid down tight. Feed him through a knothole. When he turns 16, seal up the knothole.

Some who have raised teens find it hard to decide whether to chuckle at Twain or to run out to the hardware store for a barrel and a cork! Teenagers have a knack for boxing themselves into corners of cynicism. Teens are notorious for their rebellion against authority and against the hypocrisy they see, especially in the members of their own family. They often become hypercritical of their brothers and sisters and of the adults around them.

Adolescent believers can find themselves slipping into some of these same pits as they mature in their relationships with their Lord and with members of His church. Adolescent believers can become disillusioned with their church family. They sometimes rebel against God's Law or against the authority He has placed in His church. They sometimes doubt the truths they have learned. They sometimes find a specific temptation from the past intruding into the present and trying to lure them into a future of slavery to sin.

Does all this mean God loves the adolescents in His family any less? No! Does it mean they are any less a part of that family or less valuable members of it? Not at all.

Just as few of us celebrate our 20th birthday without at least some sense of relief, few Christians emerge from spiritual adolescence unscathed. Still, as we grow spiritually, we do well to remember the blessings of adolescence: The exuberance. The zeal. The commitment. The determination. The promise. The honesty. The willingness to risk. These positive qualities come along with spiritual adolescence, too.

As the Holy Spirit uses God's Word to counsel us, His people to encourage us, and His sacraments to strengthen us, we keep on maturing. No believer arrives at a state of perfection this side of heaven. All of us live as people under construction.

But we can close our eyes at the end of each day and relax in God's peace. That peace comes from seeing our Father's fingerprints on our circumstances. That peace comes from knowing what our Savior has done for us. That peace comes from trusting the Holy Spirit's promised work in us and from the fulfillment of His purpose in our lives, whether we can always sense our transformation or not.

That, after all, is our Father's goal for each of His children. The Bible says, "Those God foreknew He also predestined to be conformed to the likeness of His Son, that He might be the firstborn among many brothers" (Romans 8:29).

Our Father nourishes our growth through His Word. As we feed on that Word, we rely on Him to produce the growth that both He and we yearn to see. We rely on Him, and not on ourselves. On the day of our spiritual graduation, that day of our home-going to heaven, we will finally see God finish the work He began here on earth. He has promised to do it:

> We know that when He [Jesus] appears, *we shall be like Him,*
> for we shall see Him as He is! (1 John 3:2, emphasis added).

What a wonder that is! What a life this new life turns out to be! God has brought us on board for this adventure and has given us a seat. But He knows what we soon learn—we'll only need the edge.

• • •

How long does it take to grow up spiritually?

As in the process of physical growth, people mature at different rates. We caution 14-year-olds to be patient as their bodies grow and develop, because every individual grows according to a unique pattern. In the same way, spiritual growth follows a unique pattern in each individual, too. Young believers need to wait patiently as they grow up in Christ. The process of spiritual growth will continue throughout life and will be finished only in eternity.

Growing up almost always hurts. Is growing up spiritually worth the pain?

Yes! Think of it! Someday we'll be like Christ Himself! And even now, we're becoming more Christlike. Bit by bit, little by little each day, the Holy Spirit is creating within us the love, the joy, the peace, the patience, the kindness, the gentleness, the goodness, the faithfulness, and the self-control of Jesus. In a very real sense, we're more like our Brother every day.

We may not notice much progress at first; we may at times even find ourselves taking some steps backwards. This should not surprise us! True, God says we are holy in His sight, even though we may look like anything but holy. We are saints (thanks to Jesus) who will struggle with sin—even become more aware of it in our lives—until our dying day. Nevertheless, over the months and years we will begin to see the growth that God is bringing about.

Like the four-year-old who discovers that at last she can open the refrigerator door to get a snack, or the fifteen-year-old who smiles to himself as he descends from his first successful slam-dunk on the basketball court, we'll catch ourselves speaking kind words or feeling peace in a crisis or understanding a principle from Scripture we haven't quite grasped before. When that happens, we'll whisper to ourselves, "I'm growing," and we'll thank our God who makes growth possible.

Does every newborn believer grow up?

No. It's sad, but true. Any human being who lives 20 years or so will almost certainly develop an adult body. Unless we suffer from some drastic genetic defect or some tragic illness befalls us, we can count on physical maturation. Spiritual growth, however, like emotional, social, or intellectual growth, can be slowed or even halted.

How can I be sure that I keep growing spiritually?

The next two chapters focus on the answer to that question.

For further reading: 1 Corinthians 3:1–16; Galatians 5:22–25

Dear Terry,

How are things going with you and your family? I'm glad the new job seems to be working out so well. I'm praying that you find a church soon, one where you will feel at home.

I didn't realize how much being with other believers meant to me until I had to work last weekend. It's the first time I'd missed a worship service since you and the others in the evangelism group called on me and led me to Christ. Both of the other two managers at my store had scheduling conflicts, so I had to open up Sunday morning. One of the joys of middle management, I guess.

I hated not being at church on Sunday. I felt like somebody snatched my weekend and took a big bite out of it. Eight or ten weeks ago if someone had told me I'd be saying something like this, I would have laughed right out loud. What a change has begun in my heart! I scarcely know myself, but I like what I've seen so far.

Your last letter, the one about growing up spiritually, helped. I understand better now what I can expect as I grow up in my faith. I'm sure there's a lot more to it than I imagine right now. But still, the more I think about what God wants to do in my life, the more excited I get.

Thinking about all that, though, has sparked another set of questions for me. Well, actually, one big question. Now that I know what to expect, I've started to wonder what God expects—what He expects from me, I mean.

I don't know how to find the answer to that question on my own, and I thought that maybe you could direct me to a specific part of the Bible or maybe another book that might help clarify God's expectations of me. I really value your advice. Thanks, Terry!

In Jesus,

Lynn

You started by the Spirit; are you now going to finish by your own effort? Galatians 3:3 (NET)

What Now? What Does God Expect of Me?

When parents bring a newborn home from the hospital, they expect to change hundreds of dirty diapers. They expect to warm up thousands of jars of pureed vegetables and to fill the Tommy Tippy cup 10 thousand times. They expect to walk the floor on dozens of sleepless nights as they nurse their little one through the teething process. They expect to wipe away countless tears and to buy countless cotton swabs.

Still, no parent expects to be mopping up strained spinach four or five decades after the ink on their child's birth certificate has dried. We expect our newborns to grow.

That, in a nutshell, is what the heavenly Father expects of newborn Christians, too. He expects us to grow. He knows that as we grow we will make some messes, and He expects us to look to Him to mop them up. He expects that we will have a ravenous spiritual appetite, and He invites us to look to Him to satisfy our hunger. He expects that we will get hurt at times, and He has high hopes that we will run to Him with our skinned knees and bruised shins.

Frank Ketchum, creator of Dennis the Menace, once described his protégé's growing up process: "Every year Dennis celebrates his sixth birthday. He blows out his candles and POOF! He's five again for another year."

We can grin a wry grin at Dennis's lack of progress. After all, he's only a cartoon character. Audiences have enjoyed his five-year-old antics for 40 years or more. But suppose Dennis were more than simply a figment of Frank Ketchum's imagination. Suppose Dennis walked around in real sneakers and held a Social Security card that had been valid for four decades. Fewer people would find themselves amused. A 45-year-old who carries a slingshot and drives his next door neighbor to distraction? Grow up, Dennis, we'd think. And rightly so.

Sad to say, the heavenly Father finds some, perhaps many, of His children still wearing spiritual diapers after they've lived in His family for decades. They celebrate spiritual birthday after spiritual birthday, blow out their candles, and POOF! They're spiritual infants all over again for yet another year.

Make no mistake, our Father loves them every bit as much as He loves those members of His family whom we call giants of faith. Still, those who live out a major portion of their spiritual lives as babies cast a short shadow of significance on the world around them. Their lives don't make much impact for their Savior, at least not a positive impact.

Perhaps most tragic of all from the heavenly Father's viewpoint, perpetual spiritual infants never experience more than the tiniest part of what Jesus died to win for them. Their Lord has spread out a smorgasbord; He has loaded His banquet table with rich and rare delicacies. But they sit back in the corner of the dining hall hoisting a baby bottle as they drink formula through a nipple.

Well then, a new believer might conclude, I'd better get busy. I'd better try as hard as I can to grow up as fast as I can. I don't want to find myself condemned to watching a Rock-a-Bye-Baby mobile dance above my spiritual crib 20 years from now.

If you're tempted to think that, stop right now. Stop and burn this truth into your heart: Your heavenly Father does not expect you to grow yourself up! Your heavenly Father does not expect you to try hard to be like Jesus!

Does your Father want you to mature spiritually? Does your Father want you to be like Christ? Yes, and yes again! That's His goal for all His children—that we'll be "conformed to the likeness of His Son" (Romans 8:29). But we'll never, ever reach that goal by trying. Or by trying hard. Or by trying harder.

One frosty evening in March of the year I turned 10, my dad stomped onto the enclosed porch of our farm house and shouted for my mom. My sisters and I stood, round eyed, as he unzipped his coveralls. He reached inside and drew out a wet, wriggling lump of wool. As he handed it to Mom, it shivered uncontrollably.

The runt of triplets born to a first-time mother, the lamb would have surely died in the cold of the sheep shed. The ewe had only enough milk for this lamb's two brothers; they thrust their sister aside whenever she nuzzled close to her mother's udder.

Elvirey—as my dad had christened her on the way to the house through the blizzard that night—spent the next several weeks snuggled down in a cardboard box next to the coal pile in our basement.

I still remember begging for the privilege of getting up at 4:00 a.m. to heat a bottle of milk and sit on the bottom basement stair to feed her.

As winter waned and the weather warmed, Mom saw to it that Elvirey moved outside. The lamb made a bed for herself near the bush where our dog slept. Whenever we filled Fibber's dog dish, we poured several handfuls of oats or ground corn into Elvirey's bowl. Dog and lamb learned the same tricks. They both came bounding up to the house at the same whistle.

Later that spring, Dad decided the time had come to return Elvirey to the flock. Not a chance. Elvirey knew beyond doubt that she did not belong with the mass of bleating dullards that occupied the pasture to which she had been banished.

Day after day she lay against the pasture fence, as close to the house and as far away from the other sheep as she could get. Fibber often trotted out to lick her nose through the bars of her prison. Whenever someone emerged from the house, Elvirey would jog to the fence, wagging her tail as she came.

Everyone in the family began to speculate about when our new pet might begin to speak—either in the canine or the human sense. The lamb had come to believe she was a dog, or perhaps a person. And despite her wool, she had spent so much time with the family, she had come to act like a member of it!

Of course, it's silly to think of a sheep actually becoming a dog, let alone a person. But then maybe not much more unreasonable than thinking that we mere, muddled, and sin-marred humans could become Christlike. Yet that's exactly the plan our Father has for us! How can it possibly happen? Our minds boggle at the possibility!

Human beings eventually become like the things they admire. We tend—most often subconsciously—to imitate the people we cherish. The Bible says, "Be imitators of God . . . as dearly loved children" (Ephesians 5:1). As we spend time with our heavenly Father, as we grow in our relationship with Him, we become more and more like Him. We begin to see things with His eyes, to feel things with His heart. Like four-year-olds clumping around in our daddy's Sunday shoes, we begin to take on His mannerisms and characteristics. In every way, we "grow up into Him who is the head, that is, Christ" (Ephesians 4:15).

• • •

Do we grow up spiritually, become more Christlike, by working at it, by trying?

No. Trying implies that we think we can grow ourselves up, that we can mature spiritually by our own effort. The Bible says, "It is God who works in you *to will* and *to act* according to His good purpose" (Philippians 2:13; emphasis added).

What's wrong with trying to improve ourselves spiritually? Don't we have to expend some effort?

Let's say you or I see something ungodly, something not at all Christlike, in our heart or lifestyle. Let's say we set out to change that attitude or behavior in ourselves. And let's say we try hard to produce the necessary change, but we find ourselves falling into the same sin again and again. Suppose we keep trying, and suppose we keep failing.

Depending on how much willpower we can muster, we may make eight or eighteen or eighty attempts. Eventually, though, we will probably give up. We'll tell ourselves (and maybe God), "I know my life needs to change, but I just can't make it happen. I guess my faith must be inferior or somehow deficient."

That attitude is really rebellion in disguise. Even so, failure in this case is better than the alternative—success.

Why is successfully overcoming sin in our own power so dangerous?

If we succeed in changing our outward behavior by our own effort, we almost inevitably begin to develop the same kind of spiritual pride that Jesus hated so much in the religious leaders of His day.

In that secret place deep inside our heart, we whisper prayers to ourselves like this: "I thank You, God, that I'm not like the spiritual wimps I see around me who can't seem to get themselves together." (See Luke 18:9–14.) Such pride robs God of the honor that belongs to Him, and it suffocates the new life God has given us.

If we don't become like Jesus by trying, how does it happen?

That's one of the truths the Bible calls "elementary teachings," the ABCs of the Christian faith (Hebrews 6:1–2). And it's the topic of the next chapter.

For further reading: 1 Peter 2:1–10; Galatians 3:1–13

Dear Terry,

Thanks for your ongoing encouragement. You say you enjoy thinking through these questions with me. I believe you, but I still think all this must seem very elementary. Then again, the elementary things are often the most important. At least that's what I keep telling the new people we hire at my store.

Many of them seem to have an attitude like this: let's hurry up and summarize all these preliminaries so we can get going with the stuff that really counts. I guess I shouldn't be so surprised that when I have to reprimand employees, it's almost always because they've forgotten to follow through on a basic procedures or because they've overlooked some elementary principle of good customer relations.

That brings me to a question that, as far as I can tell, must be one of the basics of Christianity. Since we both agree that the basics matter so much, . . . well, here goes.

If the Lord wants me to grow up to be just like Him and if trying hard to do that will only fill my heart with discouragement or pride, then how does it happen? Does God's power just sort of float around in the air and then ZAP, suddenly one day I'll wake up to find myself more like Christ? Or do I have some responsibility for my own spiritual growth? In other words, if God doesn't want me to try hard to be better, then what—if anything—does He expect me to do?

In Jesus,

Lynn

Bad news: You can't fool God.
Good news: You don't have to!

What Do I Do When I Sin?

No baby wills himself into existence. No baby gives herself life. In exactly the same way, no baby grows himself up, either. Babies don't grit their teeth and stretch their legs or arms to greater lengths. Babies don't buckle down and try hard to learn how to speak—whether English or Russian or Hmong. God has given babies life, and that life, in the normal course of things, simply unfolds and flourishes as the baby receives proper nourishment, love, and protection.

God gives each new believer spiritual life. We did not bring about our own spiritual rebirth. We cannot claim any credit for planting or germinating new life in our own hearts. What's more, none of us has the ability to grow ourselves up, spiritually speaking, either. God must protect, nurture, and nourish the new life He has begun in us if that life is to thrive and mature.

The Bible confronts us with this truth by asking a pointed question:

> You started by the Spirit; are you now going to finish by your own effort? (Galatians 3:3 NET).

No. No. A hundred times no! Thrown back on our own resources, we cannot work up the desire, the dedication, or the strength we need to obey God. Does that mean then that newborn Christians should simply settle down into a padded pew and talk themselves into being content with spiritual babyhood?

No. No. A thousand times, no! We are indeed responsible, in a very limited, but all-important way, for our spiritual growth. Our heavenly Father has spelled out that responsibility in these simple words:

> If we confess our sins, He [God] is faithful and just and will forgive us our sins and purify us from all unrighteousness (1 John 1:9).

Slow down and read those words again. Highlight them in your mind. Commit them to memory. The process the Holy Spirit gives us here will allow you to walk up to the front steps of heaven's power station, unlock the gate, and throw the master switch. God's power will flood into your life with all its light and warmth.

Dwight L. Moody once said that most believers have just enough Christianity to make them miserable. The process of repentance, the process God describes in the little verse you just read, spells the difference between a life marked by the misery of guilt-ridden failure and a life marked by steady spiritual growth. It's the first of the "elementary doctrines," the ABCs of the Christian faith (Hebrews 6:1–2). It's the key to a relationship with God that grows stronger and more satisfying as the years pass.

All Christians sin. We all disobey God at times, in fact, many times each day. The Bible tells us that until we go home to be with Jesus we will catch ourselves gossiping or swearing or lying or lusting. When we see those things in ourselves, we wince. At times, we even cry. When God leads us to see our sin as He sees it, the sight can make us sick—heart-sick. What then?

When we realize our sin, God does not ask us to grab a spiritual mop and plunge in to clean up the muck. We could never do that anyway. Instead He invites us to run to Him, to run to Him like the little children we are. He invites us to tell Him about the mess and to ask Him to mop it up.

The word the New Testament uses for *confess* comes from a Greek word that means "to say the same thing" or "to speak together." When I confess my sin, I agree with what God says about it:

- I did it.
- It was wrong.
- By my actions I have hurt myself, others, and my Lord.
- I have no excuse for my sin; it was my fault, no one else's.

When we come to our Father to do this kind of truth-telling, what happens? God could—in justice—refuse to listen to us. He could—in perfect fairness—ask the angel Gabriel to close heaven's gates to us. He could announce our sins to the entire angel army and demand a public explanation for our misdeeds. He could justly, in fact, fling us out of His sight and expel us from His family forever.

But our Lord does none of these things. Instead, He welcomes us for Jesus' sake. He gathers us in His arms and sits us down next to Him on His throne. He holds us close as He wipes away our tears of regret. He assures us that He has forgiven us and that He will never, ever count our sin against us. He floods our hearts with the relief and joy that come with His pardon.

But that's not all. He continues to flood our lives with His love by doing something so wonderful that even those who have come to know Him very well can scarcely believe it. He begins the process of "[purifying] us from all unrighteousness" (1 John 1:9).

It's as if the Holy Spirit pulls on His overalls and lowers Himself into the muck that lies waist deep in the basement of our hearts. He unstops the drain so that the sewage of our sin can gurgle away. He disinfects the walls and scrubs up the floor for us. In short, God begins the cleansing process.

With His cleansing comes true freedom—the freedom to change. To use another word-picture, after our Lord removes the guilt of our sin, He begins to peel sin's bony fingers off our throats. He tears away the blindfolds that have kept us in the dark. He opens our eyes so that we can see His love for us in the clear light of day. He lets us lean on Him for the strength we need to walk away from our captor. Free. At last.

A word the Christian church sometimes uses for forgiveness, *absolution*, comes from a Latin word that originally meant "to loose, to unshackle." As we confess our sin, God breaks into our dungeon and uses the key of His forgiveness to unlock the chains of greed, of hatred, of selfishness, of worry, of despair—all the chains of all the sins that keep us in bondage.

How sweet is the breeze of the freedom our Lord gives, blowing fresh as it does off the ocean of God's love! And how tragic that so many believers struggle under the delusion that they somehow must clean themselves up and set themselves free before God will accept them.

As we keep on using God's process for dealing with sin, as we keep on coming to kneel in confession before our Father's throne, we keep on receiving His cleansing, purifying, freeing power. All the while, He gently keeps on transforming us. We become more and more like our Brother, Jesus. As we continue to use God's process for dealing with sin, our Lord gives us more and more strength to resist Satan and his temptations. We won't reach perfect Christlikeness in this life, but if we'll be honest with God and ourselves about our sinfulness, we can expect to spot progress as we go along.

And we can expect to find ourselves struck dumb with awe at the love of our God, love at work in power for you, for me.

• • •

I've heard the word *repentance* a lot in church. What does that word mean and how does it fit into God's plan to make us like Jesus?

Everything we've talked about in this chapter so far fits into the process of repentance. Some Christians call repentance the "R word," because we all squirm at times when we need to go to God to admit failure and guilt.

But when we truly understand and believe what God offers us in this process, it can bring us a unique kind of joy, too. Even as we come to God in sorrow to confess our sin, we also come in anticipation of both His welcome and a fresh supply of His strength. What an exciting thing it can be when the Holy Spirit drives His truth deep into our hearts—the truth that even when we sin, God is on our side! (Psalm 118:5–7; Romans 8:31).

The Bible talks about this as "repentance from dead works and of faith toward God." Knowing how to use the process of repentance and knowing what God has promised to do in us and for us through it, is one of the ABCs of the Christian faith (Hebrews 6:1–2).

What is "repentance from dead works"?

Scripture uses the term "dead works" to refer to the things we try to do on our own to make up for our sins or to set ourselves free from the hold specific sins have on us (Hebrews 6:1–2). Those works are "dead" because they're empty of God's power. When we repent of dead works, we stop trying to obey in our own strength. We ask God to change in us what needs to be changed, and we trust Him to do it.

What if I confess a sin and then later find myself doing the same thing all over again?

Welcome to the normal Christian life! Sometimes, especially when an adult comes to faith in Jesus, God reaches down and seemingly flips a few switches in that new believer's heart. The newborn Christian may stop swearing overnight. Or the person may lose all desire to abuse drugs or alcohol. God sovereignly and supernaturally puts the brakes on specific, particularly dangerous sins.

But that doesn't always happen, and it never happens with every sin in the new believer's life. Our struggle with sin is ongoing, lifelong. We will often find ourselves repeating sins after we've confessed them. Sometimes, to our shame and disgust, that will happen again and again.

What do I do if I find myself trapped in a specific sin?

First of all, you need to remember that repeated sin does not shock God. He knows your weaknesses. He knows the hardness of human hearts. He knows just how deeply sin can sink its fangs into us and how enticingly Satan can sugar-coat his temptations.

That does not mean that defeat is inevitable. God has given us the process of repentance as His medicine, as His remedy for the sin in our lives. He invites, urges, and even commands us to use it and to keep on using it.

Our Doctor won't grow angry at us for taking the medicine He Himself has prescribed. We can't overdose on it. Even if you find that you need to confess the same sin five times every five minutes, you can do so confident that God's forgiveness and also His cleansing power will always be there for you.

How often can I ask God for help with my sin?

Not only *can* you ask for help as often as you need it, you *must* do so unless you want to live a life of misery and defeat. There is no other path toward true Christlikeness. Think of it this way. Someone who sets out to break down a concrete wall will seldom see results with the first blow. The sledge hammer may rise and fall a hundred times, five hundred times, a thousand times. Sooner or later, though, the wall will crumble.

As you continue by God's grace to use God's process—the process of repentance—the fortresses of sin that Satan has set up in your heart will eventually fall. Some sooner. Some later. But no matter what, you need not feel discouraged or give up. God is on your side! He will stay right there in the middle of your struggle with you. He's promised to do that and He keeps His Word.

Does the Bible talk about other ABCs of the Christian life?

Yes. Hebrews 6 goes on to mention several other foundational principles. In addition to "repentence for acts that lead to death," the writer says, "Let us leave the elementary teachings about Christ and go on to maturity, not laying again the foundation of . . . faith in God, instruction about baptisms, the laying on of hands, the resurrection of the dead, and eternal judgment." (Hebrews 6:1–2).The next chapter reviews them.

For further reading: Psalm 32; Romans 8:1–2

Dear Terry,

Wow, it was great to chat with you on the phone yesterday! You're right—brothers and sisters in Christ can be closer than people in our own earthly family. I can't believe what a lift our conversation gave me.

I've decided to ask Pastor Bartlett about baptizing me, just as you suggested. I wish you and your family could come back for the service, but I understand. After all (and as you keep on reminding me), Wisconsin is halfway across the continent from here.

By the way, I'd love to take a winter vacation this year. I've always wanted to learn cross-country skiing. You now enjoy the perfect location for that, and you've said I'm always welcome. (You may live to eat your words!)

Anyway, I've been mulling over some of what you said yesterday about Baptism—what it means and what God does in it. I must admit that I've always thought of it as some sort of religious ritual—you know, some kind of pious ceremony.

You surely blew that idea out of the water! But after I hung up, I had the distinct impression that it's not magical either. So now I'm not sure what to think. My head won't stop spinning.

Do you suppose you could put some of this in writing so I could think it through more thoroughly?

Gotta run, Terry. Thanks again! You and your family remain in my prayers.

In Jesus,

Lynn

If anyone is in Christ, he is a new creation; the old has gone, the new has come! 2 Corinthians 5:17

What Does God Think of Me?

Who are you? Who are you really? Suppose you entered a contest: "Describe yourself in 25 words or less." What words would you pick?

Doctor? Or lawyer? Or town police chief
Rich man? Poor man? Butcher of beef?
Scholar or drop-out or just-average Joe?
Marathon runner? Or couch potato?
Professional woman? Stay-at-home dad?
Perpetually happy? Or habitually sad?
Just getting started? Or recently retired?
Always energetic? Or twice-a-year fired?
Life full of meaning? Or just bored to tears?
Who's the you that you've become
After all of these years?

Who's the you that you've become? What 25 words would you use to answer that question? Would your list include the description "delight-bringer"? Or "majestic one"? Ridiculous, you say?

Well, how about "saint"? Or "one of God's crown jewels"?

Maybe you would feel more comfortable with describing your identity in terms of your relationships—"brother or sister of Jesus," for instance? Or "heir of heaven"? Or maybe "ambassador for Christ"? You are all these things, you know. And more!

Imagine that you could eavesdrop on a conversation or two in heaven. Would you expect to see God dancing and hear Him shouting for joy—over you? Can you imagine Him leaning over the celestial balcony to see what's happening here on earth, and then hear Him as He turns back over His shoulder to shout, "Gabriel! Michael! Come here! Look! Look at My children! Do you see how they've grown? They're more like their Brother every day. Aren't they delightful?"

Does that picture startle you? Do you feel your brow furl into a frown of skepticism? Then think about what our Lord has said about us:

[God's people] will sparkle in His land like jewels in a crown. How attractive and beautiful they will be! (Zechariah 9:16–17).

The Lord your God is with you, He is mighty to save. He will take great delight in you, . . . He will rejoice over you with singing (Zephaniah 3:17).

For [God] chose us in [Christ] before the creation of the world to be holy and blameless in His sight. In love He predestined us to be adopted as His sons through Jesus Christ (Ephesians 1:4–5).

Speaking through King David, the Holy Spirit said:

As for the saints who are in the earth, They are the majestic ones in whom is all my delight (Psalm 16:3 NASB).

Do you hear your Father sing for joy? He does, you know, every time He thinks of you. And He thinks about you all the time! (Psalm 139:1–4; 17–18).

We've all heard the lie told by the world system around us—you are what you do. Of course, our trade, our occupation, our career, our lifestyle truly do matter to our heavenly Father. But after we become a part of the family of God, our identity no longer comes just from those things. In fact, it no longer comes primarily from those things.

In Christ we have a new identity. We've been adopted into the family of a great and loving King. We belong. And not as step-children relegated to the attic when company comes. Jesus once said:

As the Father has loved Me, so have I loved you (John 15:9).

How much does the Father love Jesus? That's how much love our big Brother has for us. We're full members of God's family, our adoption papers, as it were, sealed at our Baptism.

Every time we take a shower, every time we open the kitchen tap to get a drink, every time we wash the dishes or do the laundry, we can remember the moment that God touched us with water and His Word to claim us as His own.

God speaks in Baptism, and God's Word carries with it the power to accomplish what He has said. What does God say? Romans 6 explains that in Baptism
- we die with Christ;
- we are buried with Christ;
- we are raised with Christ; and

- we live in Christ.

Because of what God has done for us—in Christ—and because of what God has done in us—in our Baptism—we can consider ourselves dead to sin. Writing in the context of Baptism, Paul encouraged his readers in Rome: "Count yourselves dead to sin but alive to God in Christ" (Romans 6:11).

"Mark it down in your ledger," Paul would say if he had written in English rather than in the Greek of the New Testament. "It's a truth you can take to the bank. Cash in on it!" In Baptism, God gives us a new identity and with it, a new freedom. He has released us from slavery to sin. These gifts are so real and so precious that anyone who audits heaven's books must, without question, recognize them as valid.

Hebrews 6 calls Baptism one of the elementary doctrines, one of the ABCs of the Christian faith. Even so, the gifts God gives us in it are so great that while we live on this side of heaven, Baptism will always remain something of a mystery to us. Mysterious as it is, though, one thing is for certain—in Baptism, it's God who acts, God who gives. We simply receive and rejoice.

Our minds are too small to grasp and hold the whole truth of what happens in Baptism. But the Bible makes it clear that in Baptism our identity changes. We are no longer what we were. We are no longer what we do. And, praise God, we are no longer what we have done.

Now, Christ's right standing with God has become our own; we have inherited Jesus' righteousness. We're alive from the dead! Our sins are forgiven. We are no longer spiritual zombies stumbling through life as if through a grade B movie. Our citizenship in the land of the living dead has been revoked. No longer must we dance to Satan's tune as he pulls our strings. Make no mistake—we once lived that way, but no longer!

And that's not the end of what heaven's probate court has awarded us. We have inherited literally everything that belongs to Christ Jesus! We have become His co-heirs (Romans 8:17). We have fallen heir to all the riches of the universe:

- The right to call ourselves God's own children
- The complete forgiveness of all our sins—past, present, and future

- The guarantee of God's power to live as His chosen, dearly loved people
- The privilege of entering God's throne-room to present our requests and to know we have been heard
- The protection of heaven's holy angels
- The certainty of life with Christ now and forever—a certainty that nothing, not even physical death, can snatch away

At Baptism, God touches us personally and declares before all heaven and hell, "This one is mine!"

Who are you really? Doctor? Stay-at-home dad? Professional woman? Marathon runner? Couch potato? Perhaps. But how those labels pale beside your true identity—baptized child of God, heir of heaven.

• • •

Hebrews 6:1–2 lists other ABCs of the faith. One of these is "the laying on of hands." What is that?

This phrase may refer to the practice of blessing believers during the Sacrament of Baptism. In other places in the New Testament, these same words are used to describe a practice God gave His church to confer His blessing on people as He sets them aside for special service in His kingdom—pastors, for instance. Something real and powerful happens as the Lord, through His church, blesses His servants in this way. See, for example, 1 Timothy 4:14 and 2 Timothy 1:6.

God gives His people pastors—shepherds—and then gives those pastors the gifts they need in order to care for His people.

The last two ABC doctrines listed in Hebrews 6 are "the resurrection of the dead" and "eternal judgment." How would you explain these?

All of the leaders of all the world's religions throughout all of recorded history have eventually died. Their followers have buried them, and their bodies have turned to dust. All, that is,except one. The garden tomb of Joseph of Arimathea once held the dead body of Jesus Christ. For three days it looked as though evil and death had won. But Jesus' body lies dead no longer. As the apostle Paul so eloquently thunders, "But now Christ is risen from the dead!"

Then the apostle adds, "and has become the firstfruits of those who have fallen asleep" (1 Corinthians 15:20 NKJV). Christ rose first; His brothers and sisters—that's us—will follow.

During the time the early Christian church endured the horrors of persecution, believers referred to the day each martyr died as "the day of his victory," the "day of her victory." In a very real sense, each of us who belongs to Christ Jesus can think of the day of our death as the day of our victory, too. That's the day we receive our inheritance in all its fullness. That's the day we become fully Christlike:

> Dear friends, now we are children of God, and what we will be has not yet been made known. But we know that when [Christ Jesus] appears, we shall be like Him, for we shall see Him as He is (1 John 3:2).

On the day of resurrection, our Savior will call our bodies from the grave. Our Judge will publicly confirm the verdict that has already been rendered in heaven's courtroom—Not Guilty! Our Lord will take us with Him to enjoy the richness of our inheritance in Christ. We will live forever in our Father's home—forever free from sin, forever free from sickness, forever free from pain and sorrow, forever free from tears, forever beyond the clutches of Satan and of death. What an inheritance! What a Savior!

For further reading: Romans 6:1–14; 1 Corinthians 15

Dear Terry,

I'm still in the process of absorbing all you've had to say about the ABCs of Christianity. It may take a while! It's such a different approach—focusing on what God is doing and has done for me in Jesus instead of focusing on what God demands I do for Him. I guess I always had the impression that being a Christian meant following a long list of rules. Wow! Was that ever wrong!

From everything you've said and written, it's clear to me now that being a Christian means being in a relationship with God, a relationship that can only exist because of what Jesus did for me on the cross.

I'm coming to realize that this relationship is the most important relationship in my life. If that's true—and I believe it is—then I wonder exactly how that relationship deepens and matures.

If I wanted to cultivate a new human friendship, I'd ask my friend out to lunch or to see a movie with me. But how do I "take God out to the movies," so to speak? How do I get to know Him better?

Don't take this the wrong way, but I hope you don't say, "Read the Bible." I realize that must be part of it. Everyone says so. But I've tried, and it's just too much for me. I need to grow up more first, I guess. But for now I just don't seem to be able to understand it or stick with it.

Thanks for listening!

In Jesus,

Lynn

How Can I Get to Know God Better?

Imagine yourself opening your mailbox this afternoon. Imagine yourself sorting through the bills and junk mail. Imagine that as you shuffle the envelopes, one suddenly begins to glow. Imagine the advertising circulars dropping to the floor as you stare at the return address on the mysterious envelope: Heaven. This letter has your name on it. It's come to you directly from your Father. How long would it take you to tear open the flap and begin to read?

Sometimes believers struggle with Bible reading because they forget or perhaps have never really known what the Bible truly is. They don't realize that God has written a letter, a letter from His heart to your heart.

We may find it hard to believe, but our God *wants* to communicate with us. He wants us to know how much He loves us—personally. He wants to tell us of His dreams and hopes for us personally.

Some people read the Bible to learn facts and history. We may find those things interesting. But God has not given us His Word so that we can chalk up thousands of points in some celestial game of Biblical Jeopardy by remembering the name of the fifth king to rule Judah after Rehoboam! God gives us His Word because He so wants to nourish the relationship He has established with us.

An old children's hymn begins:

> Deep and wide,
> Deep and wide,
> God's love is flowing
> Deep and wide.

How true that is. And how eagerly our Father invites us to come swim in His love! To come immerse ourselves in the wonder of it! To come sit right next to Him on His throne and let Him fill our hearts with it. God wants that for us every time we read the Bible.

If that's to happen, though, we need to approach our Bible reading in that way, with that expectation. Here are some hints you may find helpful:

- Talk to the Holy Spirit as you begin to read God's Word. Ask Him to help you get to know Him better as you read.

- Continue to talk to your Lord as you read. Ask Him to explain the things you don't understand.
- Let your Savior examine your heart as you read. Let Him shine His light into the dark corners. Confess the sin He shows you.
- Look for your Father's words of forgiveness, of absolution, of freedom. Look for His words of promise, hope, and victory. Thank Him for Jesus, your Savior and friend.
- Ask the Holy Spirit to help you grasp the truths He wants to use in your life—not just sometime in the future, but during the next few hours and days.
- Mark verses that speak to your heart in a particularly powerful way. Write brief notes to yourself in the margin. Put question marks next to passages you don't understand. Personalize your Bible—it's God's love letter to you!
- Choose one or two verses a week and commit them to memory. Write each verse on its own note card and tack it to your refrigerator, your dashboard, or your desk at work. Read and reread it. Let the truths of God's Word soak down into the depths of your heart.
- Before you finish your devotional time, ask God to bring His Word back to your mind often during the day, especially at times when you need His comfort, wisdom, or strength. He's promised to do that. Speaking about God's words, the writer of Proverbs says: "Bind them upon your heart forever; fasten them around your neck. When you walk, they will guide you; when you sleep, they will watch over you; when you awake, they will speak to you. For these commands are a lamp, this teaching is a light, and the corrections of discipline are the way to life" (Proverbs 6:21–23).

Listen to your Lord as He speaks to you in His Word. Talk to Him about what He says. Then stand back and watch. Watch your relationship grow as He brings about changes in your heart and life.

• • •

What makes the Bible such a uniquely life-changing book?

The Bible is God's Word. When God speaks, things happen. God spoke at the beginning of time, for example, and the universe sprang into existence. St. Paul wrote, "I am not ashamed of the Gospel, because it is the power of God for the salvation of everyone who believes" (Romans 1:16).

The Greek word God led Paul to use for *power* is the word from which we get our English words *dynamite* and *dynamo*. The Gospel is dynamic. It carries with it God's power to change the hearts it touches. We can expect God's Word to change us, to bring salvation—wholeness—to our hearts and lives.

Why do some people read Scripture and not get anything out of it?

Note what Paul said: The Gospel "is the power of God for the salvation of everyone who believes." Those to whom the Holy Spirit has given the gift of faith find the Holy Scriptures a rich treasure chest of hope, comfort, and encouragement. Those who approach God's Book with skeptical hearts, not expecting God to speak to them in it, will not hear from Him. As Jesus once said, "My sheep listen to My voice; I know them, and they follow Me" (John 10:27).

Will sincere Christians ever have trouble motivating themselves to read the Bible?

Yes. When Jesus raised His friend Lazarus from the dead (John 11), Lazarus came out of the tomb, his burial clothes still clinging to him. Jesus has raised us from spiritual death and has given us life, too—eternal life. A real change has taken place in our hearts. We have a new identity. Still, sin, like burial clothes, clings to us. Because that's true, we are often reluctant to meet with God by reading His Word. We will at times find ourselves fighting the urge to do something else instead.

Why does Satan want to keep God's people from studying the Scriptures?

Satan shudders every time one of God's people opens the Book. He knows—even better than we do—the power of God's dynamite. He has seen his stratagems blown into a million pieces time and time again as believers at all stages of spiritual maturity have used the Word to overcome him. Satan worries about that happening, and he works hard to prevent it. He distracts us, and he tries to muddle our priorities, tempting us to place our Lord and His Word somewhere near the bottom of each day's to-do list.

Suppose someone who doesn't know much about the Bible wants to start reading it. What's a good place to begin?

Probably not at the beginning. God alone knows how many Christians have begun with Genesis, planning to read straight through the Bible much like they would read a novel. Most often, they get to some of the ceremonies and regulations in Exodus and Leviticus and give up.

Remember that the Bible is not really a single book, but rather a library of 66 separate books. Someone new to Bible reading will do well to begin by reading one of the first four New Testament books (the gospels)—Matthew, Mark, Luke, or John. Of those, Mark is probably the easiest to understand. After the gospels, you might dig into some of Paul's shorter letters—Philippians, for instance.

How many verses or chapters might a new Bible reader study in one sitting?

Set realistic goals. Sometimes you might read a single verse and hear God speaking so powerfully that you simply want to read and reread those words until you feel confident you've grasped what He's saying to you. At other times, you may read a whole chapter or even two. Don't race the clock to see how far you can get in a set amount of time. Aim at getting to know God better, not at setting a new land-speed record for pages covered.

How much time do I need to set aside for Bible reading?

Don't expect a program entitled "Getting to Know God in Three Minutes a Day" to turn you into a spiritual giant. Our culture would like to believe otherwise, but things that are worthwhile take time, and spiritual growth is worthwhile.

I find that if I spend less than 20 minutes or so, I walk away from my devotions disappointed. It often takes 10 minutes to clear my mind and to let God open my heart so I can hear what He wants to tell me.

On the other hand, some Christians put off reading the Scriptures until they can "devote quality time" to it. They wait until they have an hour or more to spend. To no one's surprise, except perhaps their own, they don't study the Bible very often.

Ask God to help you find a 20–30 minute slot you can spend with Him on a daily basis. Ink that time in on your calendar and keep your appointment with your Lord as conscientiously as you would keep any other important appointment.

What do I do if I don't feel like reading the Bible?

God invites us to meditate on His Word. In fact, He commands us to do that. Not doing it and, in fact, not wanting to do it is sin. If you've read this far, you know what to do with sin—confess it (without making excuses for yourself) and ask God to cleanse you of it.

Then act on His promise to work in you *to will* and *to do* what He commands (Philippians 2:13). Ask Him to make you hungry for His Word. Ask Him to give you the desire He wants you to have.

After you've developed the habit of daily Bible reading, by God's grace, your day will feel incomplete without it. You'll miss spending time with your heavenly Father on those days you don't get to it.

Should I mark my Bible? What kinds of things might I mark?

Many Christians personalize their Bibles. Some, for instance, use highlighting pens. If you go this route, choose markers that won't bleed through the pages. Other believers use colored pencils and mark passages that deal with specific topics. Here's one possible color scheme you may find helpful as you study:

- Red—verses that promise God's forgiveness for our sins
- Blue—verses that spell out God's other promises to us
- Orange—verses that talk about becoming Christlike
- Gray—verses that tell about Satan and his schemes
- Purple—verses about Christ's return and the end times
- Pink—verses about money and about Christian giving
- Green—verses about the church and about our part in it
- Yellow—verses that seem especially worshipful or that tell something important about what God is like

For further reading: 2 Timothy 3:10–17; Psalm 119:9–16

Dear Terry,

Thought you'd like to know—I bought a set of markers to use as I read my Bible. It works! But the biggest difference is talking the ideas over with Jesus while I study. You're right—the Bible is God's Word to me personally! It's great!

Finding time each day to read and pray, though, wasn't easy. I finally settled on early morning. I've started getting up about 30 minutes earlier than I had been and then stopping for breakfast at Hardees on my way in to work. I felt a bit conspicuous at first—reading the Bible in public like that, I mean. But gradually it's become a more and more comfortable part of my routine (even though I still groan as loudly as ever when the alarm goes off!).

My time with the Lord has become an island of peace in my day, and wow, do I ever need it! My schedule has gotten more and more crunched over the past few months.

I used to run a lot of errands on Sunday morning. You know, shop for groceries, have the oil changed in my car, do the laundry, and all that. Don't panic—I'm not thinking about giving up church! But I don't quite know how to divide up my week anymore.

The biggest time crunch comes in that I find myself spending more and more time with my Christian friends. Some of the people at church have invited me to join their home Bible study group after the adult class with pastor ends. I want to fit in at Immanuel. But I can't keep up.

How do you do it, Terry? How do you juggle work, church, family—and still have time for yourself? How do you decide what to do and what to leave undone?

Thanks again, Terry, for your help with the Bible reading!
In Jesus,

Lynn

*I have all the time I need to accomplish those things God has
for me to do today.*

What Do I Do When I Can't Do It All?

Maybe you've run across some of the same time management
articles that have crossed my desk. You know the ones. You'd recognize them by the tidy, multi-colored circles that purport to picture
a balanced lifestyle. Eight hours for sleep—one-third of the pie.
Eight hours for work—one-third of the pie. One hour for exercise—
one sliver of the pie. Two hours for social activities—a bigger sliver.
And so it goes.

If life is a cherry pie, many of us find ourselves slicing the
pieces thinner and thinner. We catch ourselves looking for faster
ways to do just about everything. We strain to save 10 minutes here
and 15 minutes there as we frantically pack more and more activity
into each of our days. Trouble is, as we slice the pie into slivers, the
cherries tend to fall out. Our joy and our sense of purpose drop
away.

Time management articles written by Christians sometimes take
a different tack. They retain the pie theory, but like pastry chefs
from a foreign culture, they suggest we slice our pie to form three
concentric circles. They tell us to label the central circle "Jesus,"
the middle ring "others," and the outer ring "self." They assure us
that this way of setting priorities—Jesus first, others second, ourselves last—will bring us true contentment.

It sounds terrific. How spiritual and self-sacrificing! But then
reality barges in the front door, picks up the pie, and proceeds to
pitch it at us. Before we know what's hit us, we're wiping whipped
cream off our eyelids.

Whether the conflict comes that dramatically or not, anyone
who follows the Jesus—Others—Yourself (J-O-Y) model with much
commitment will surely encounter frustration in deciding how to
apply it. Does putting Jesus first mean that I spend all my time reading the Bible? If so, what happens to my job or to my family? Does
putting myself last mean I can't take time to jog or to see a movie?
What does it mean to care for others when the needs of person A
conflict with the needs of person B?

Pious as the J-O-Y model sounds, it just doesn't work. If we look at the "others" around us with our eyes even half open, we'll spot limitless needs. The brokenness of sin insures that there will always be more requests than resources. More requests than resources, that is, if we if we expect ourselves to meet every need we see.

Whether we slice our time into traditional wedges or into exotic circles, whether God's slice ends up being generous or meager, He still gets only a slice. And that's not what He wants. He wants, you see, the whole pie—the crust, the cherries, and even the ice cream on top!

Does this sound like tyranny? Perhaps so. But regardless of how it sounds to our tone-deaf, sin-infected ears, it is in fact the beginning of true freedom.

God's Old Testament people lived under the tyrant's boot as slaves in Egypt for centuries. All their time—24 hours of every day, 10,080 minutes of every week, 31,536,000 seconds of every year—belonged to their slave masters. Through Moses, God came to Israel's rescue. God set them free. Then He gave them instructions about how to use their freedom. Among those instructions, came this command:

> Six days you shall labor and do all your work, but the seventh day is a Sabbath to the Lord your God. On it you shall not do any work, neither you, nor your son or daughter. . . . Remember that *you were slaves in Egypt* and that the Lord your God brought you out of there with a mighty hand and an outstretched arm. Therefore the Lord your God has commanded you to observe the Sabbath day (Deuteronomy 5:13–15; emphasis added).

Note the past tense of that all-important verb—"you *were* slaves." Not long before, their slavery had defined them, had identified them. But no longer. God had freed them from all that.

And now, in love, God told His people, "Take a day off. Once a week, stop all your busyness. Stop your mad dash toward wealth. Leave the plow in the field. Unharness the ox. Stop all the planting. Stop all the harvesting. Don't cook. Don't clean the house. Don't heat up the kiln to fire your pottery. Enjoy your family. Enjoy your friends. Enjoy spending time with Me. You were slaves. But now you're free. You're My people, My heirs. Live like the King's kids you've become."

Of course, legalists among the Israelites eventually managed to turn God's day of rest into a new slavery, a new tyranny. But that perversion doesn't destroy God's intention. The Sabbath was His gift of love to ancient Israel. Keeping God's Sabbath day gave the Israelites a reputation for laziness among other ancient peoples. Those from other cultures who saw God's people work six days and then rest on the seventh day shook their heads in disgust. What a waste of time all this resting and worship were, the go-getters of that day thought.

You see, though, God gave the Sabbath law because He wanted to teach His people a critical truth: All their time belonged to Him. In fact, everything they were and everything they had belonged to Him. Lock, stock, and barrel. Body, soul, and spirit.

Those who worshiped other gods had to live by the philosophy "Heaven helps those who help themselves." The pagans had to care for their own needs. They had to use their time in sweating and slaving service to idols of silver and gold. (Does this sound familiar?)

God's people had once lived in shackles, just like the pagans. Once upon a time they, too, had groveled at the feet of slave masters. But now they belonged to the living God, the God who does only good things for His people. They could trust this God with their lives; He would care for them. They could trust Him with their time; He would make it possible for them to do the things that needed doing in each new day.

Work was important, but so was rest. Possessions were important, but people were more important. And each person's relationship with the Lord was most important of all. That's why God pleaded with each of His Old Testament people, "My son, [My daughter,] give Me your heart" (Proverbs 23:26).

Our Lord makes that same plea to His people today. God wants my heart, my whole heart. And when He has my heart, He has my life and He has my time as well.

But just exactly what does that mean as I slice up next week's calendar or serve up today's activities on a plate with a dollop of whipped cream?

Simply this. As God works in me, I come to see that all my time belongs to God. As I set each day's priorities, as I decide how to spend each hour, I can ask myself, "What would Jesus do?" Then I can ask my heavenly Father for the courage and power I need to do just exactly that. Because the Holy Spirit is at work in my life, I'm growing up to become more and more like Christ. As that happens, the ways I choose to use my time will reflect more and more exactly my Lord's priorities.

It's curious. I give the whole pie to my Savior. He receives it, blesses it—and then, wonder of wonders, gives it back to me! And as He does, He changes it. He transforms it into something more delectable, more beautiful than I ever believed possible. My use of time brings me joy. And as I share my time, I bring joy to my Lord's heart and joy into the lives of others.

• • •

Does God care about how I use my time?

If I belong to Christ, I can no longer think of time as "my time." Every minute of every day belongs to God who gives time to me as a gift. And yes, God does care how I use it. Listen to what St. Paul wrote about that:

> Whatever you do, whether in word or deed, do it all in the name of the Lord Jesus, giving thanks to God the Father through Him (Colossians 3:17).

> Whatever you do, work at it with all your heart, as working for the Lord, not for men, since you know that you will receive an inheritance from the Lord as a reward. It is the Lord Christ you are serving (Colossians 3:23–24).

> So whether you eat or drink or whatever you do, do it all for the glory of God (1 Corinthians 10:31).

I'm afraid that if all my time belongs to God, I'll lose myself—the real me, I mean. Won't that happen?

No. You'll discover the real you, perhaps for the first time. You'll discover the you that's becoming more like Christ. Remember, the Lord Jesus did not lead a ho-hum life. His heavenly Father led Him into terrific relationships and mind-boggling opportunities to help others. And the heavenly Father gave Jesus all the support and all the power He needed to do what God wanted done. The heavenly Father wants to do that very same thing for us as well.

How did Jesus set priorities for His life?

The New Testament paints an attractive picture of the Savior. Jesus loved people; He loved to be with them. And people loved to be with Jesus. Can't you just see His eyes dance with excitement as He told hurting people about the Father's love? as He comforted them? as He taught them? as He healed their sicknesses and pain?

Jesus gave Himself to people. He led a busy—but balanced—life. Scripture never shows Him frantic. Nor panicked. Nor even in a hurry. He often withdrew from the crowds to pray. He often got into Peter's fishing boat and pulled away from the demands of people on shore so He and His disciples could rest.

How did Jesus balance work and service with rest and time for relationships?

Jesus listened to His Father. Jesus did what His Father wanted Him to do, and He used God's power to do it. He once said, "It is the Father, living in Me, who is doing His work" (John 14:10).

Jesus looked to the Father to set His priorities. That's why toward the end of His life Christ could pray, "I have finished the work You have given Me to do" (John 17:4 NKJV).

Had all the sick in Galilee been healed? No.

Had everyone in the Roman Empire heard the Good News of forgiveness through the cross? No.

But Jesus had finished that part of the work the Father had set aside for Him.

How can I be less frantic and more Christlike as I manage my time and my life?

Try this. As the alarm rings tomorrow morning, pray:

> Lord, show me what You would do today if You walked around in my shoes.

Then trust Him to answer that prayer and to give you the power you need to respond as He opens opportunities to you.

Act in love and concern for others, for yourself, and for your Lord. Not because you have to. But because you'll want to. And you get to.

For further reading: Psalm 90; Colossians 3:23–24

Dear Terry,

I'm feeling so exasperated I can hardly write. I just got home from work. My manager told me today that we shouldn't expect a raise for another six months—at least. It's been a year and a half since the last one, and I'm putting in probably a third more hours than I was back then. What a disappointment!

Then I got home and opened the mail. Here's where the exasperation comes in. Out fell four—count 'em—four requests for donations to one worthy cause or another. It seems like the more a person gives, the more people expect. My name must be on dozens of direct mail "hit lists."

Since I've started attending Immanuel, I've shifted some of what I used to give to charities over to church. Still, the please-give-we're-in-a-crisis letters keep coming from all over the map. If I gave even five dollars to everyone who wants a piece of my pay check, I wouldn't be able to pay my rent!

I don't want to sound stingy, Terry, but my landlord and the utility companies won't be impressed by a stack of receipts from charitable causes. I want to give, but I'd like to know how much. And I'd like some help in deciding where to give it. What does God expect? Five percent? Ten? More? Less? Does giving to the Heart Fund count?

I'm going out for a walk. Maybe I can blow off some of this pent-up steam. I wish I understood why this bugs me so much.

Thanks, Terry!

Lynn

God doesn't care if we have things;
He just doesn't want our things to have us.

How Does God Want Me to Use Money?

Once upon a time, not long ago, the Internal Revenue Service received an envelope that contained some cash and this handwritten note:

> I can't sleep. Here's $250. If I still can't sleep, I'll send you the other $250.

Guilty taxpayers often send money to the IRS anonymously in an attempt to salve their consciences. Tax officials can't tell whether or not it cures insomnia.

Some Christians mistakenly think of Christian giving in much the same way as guilt-ridden taxpayers. Some even refer to the money they give as "church dues" or "pew tax." Terms like these reveal the thoughts and attitudes of their hearts. Somehow, these people feel, God has found a way to get His bony hands on their wallet.

Christians with this attitude may worry their way through some sleepless nights. What will happen if they fail to give? Or if they fail to give enough? They know they probably won't wind up in prison as they would if the government convicted them of tax evasion.

But they stew about the possibility that God may find a way to weaken their financial position. Maybe the engine of their car will blow up. Maybe the heat exchanger on their furnace will crack. Maybe the landlord will raise the rent. Maybe the stock market will collapse and bury their life savings in the rubble.

Does God get mad at us if we fail to give? Or if we fail to give enough? How much is enough? What does He expect of us?

"All the Earth Is Mine"

Imagine the leaders of your local congregation nailing the church doors shut and hanging up a sign that says, "Stop coming to worship. Stop bringing your money." Ludicrous, you say? Then listen to what God told His people through His spokesperson, a prophet named Malachi, about 400 years before Jesus was born:

"Oh, that one of you would shut the temple doors, so that you would not light useless fires on My altar! I am not pleased with you," says the Lord Almighty, "and I will accept no offering from your hands" (Malachi 1:10).

Why would the Lord say such things? Because the worship and the gifts the people offered Him amounted to only so much ritual. They came to worship because they felt compelled. They brought sacrifices because they felt they must. How much would you treasure a gift someone gave you, not out of love and respect, but from a heart filled with the kind of compulsion or fear most people feel when they think about the tax collector?

When we pay our taxes, most of us experience at least fleeting patriotism and thankfulness that we live in a nation in which we enjoy so many freedoms and opportunities. Still, most of us look for as many loopholes as possible. We may even hire an accountant to find more legitimate deductions for us.

The people to whom Malachi wrote apparently had even less regard for their God than they had for their king! They turned over rocks looking for ways to get by as cheaply as they could when they brought their gifts to their Lord. God responded to all this by shouting, "STOP! I don't want your offerings. Keep your so-called gifts."

Malachi's generation wasn't the first to struggle with the challenge of giving. Several centuries earlier, God had spoken to His people through Asaph about the same heart-attitude:

Hear, O My people, . . . and I will testify against you: I am God, your God. . . . I have no need of a bull from your stall or of goats from your pens, for every animal of the forest is Mine and the cattle on a thousand hills. . . . If I were hungry, I would not tell you, for the world is Mine, and all that is in it (Psalm 50:7–12).

God's people had apparently grown so defensive and so hardened in heart that it had short-circuited their logic. "Think!" God tells them, in essence. "I'm God. The Creator of the universe. Remember Me? I don't need the livestock you're raising. If I wanted to barbecue a few steaks, I wouldn't have to call you to cater My picnic!"

What a foolish notion!

God's people today would never fall into such ridiculous thinking, would they? Of course, you know the answer to that. You know we do. We may not literally latch the barn door to keep God away from our herd of prime Angus. We may not moan and groan in the pretense that we've endured a lean harvest. But we may find ourselves a little miffed at God when we pass the offering plate to the person sitting next to us in the worship service. We may find ourselves tempted to give, to the penny, the amount of money that will let us fall asleep with a clear conscience.

A Tithe?

Some Christian teachers hammer home the idea that God demands 10 percent of our income—of our adjusted gross income, that is. These teachers and their listeners might be surprised to learn that 10 percent is not enough. God won't settle for 10 percent of our money. Nor for 25 percent. He won't be satisfied with even 50 percent of our income. Our Lord wants it all. One hundred percent.

Astonishing? Unreasonable? Not really. Not when you remember that He created everything that exists in the first place. All the gold in all the world's mines. All the oil in all the world's oil reserves. All the diamonds. All the forests. All the oceans. All the mountains. All the stars that dot the heavens. He made it all. He owns it all. He holds the title deed, free and clear.

The things we at times so arrogantly claim as our own do not, in the final analysis, really belong to us. They're on loan to us from our Father. He lets us use them. The place we live. The clothes we wear. The body we clothe. The money we earn and our ability to earn it. The air we breathe. He lets us use all these things. The great English poet, John Donne, wrote about this paradox:

> We are God's tenants here,
> and yet here He, our landlord,
> pays us rents—
> not yearly, nor quarterly,
> but hourly and quarterly;
> every minute He renews His mercy.

God fills our lives with good things. And what's more, He wants us to enjoy them. He takes pleasure in bringing us delight. As we enjoy His gifts, He wants us to learn to take good care of them. He wants us to learn to manage the resources He gives us. After all, He takes excellent care of His creation, and as we grow more and more like Him, we ourselves will become better and better caretakers of the blessings He has entrusted to us.

Take special note of the paragraph you just read. Read it again. The four principles imbedded in it form the foundation you need as you grow to become more and more like Jesus in the financial/material part of your life:

- God loves to give.
- God loves to see us enjoy His gifts.
- God wants to help us learn to manage His gifts with excellence.
- Part of managing well involves using the resources God has given us to spread the Good News of Jesus and to meet other people-needs.

As we allocate the resources God has given us, we need to keep asking ourselves one powerful question: Where's my heart? If God has your heart, then He has your money. All of it. If God has your heart, then He has your time. All of it. If God has your heart, then He has your career. All of it. If God has your heart, then He has your relationships. All of them.

A Litmus Test

Maybe you remember litmus paper from junior high science class. Acids turned the paper pink. Bases turned the paper blue. No matter how much you dilute an acid, you can't fool litmus paper. Even the weakest acid will show up as acid in a litmus test. And no matter how much you dilute a base, you can't fool litmus paper. Even the weakest base will show up as a base in a litmus test.

Think of opportunities to give as a kind of litmus test. Every time you or I sit down to write out a check to a Christian ministry or to a secular charity, we need to run a quick heart test. We need to ask, "Am I giving gladly? Without nursing a grudge? Am I giving because I think God will love me a little more if I ante up? Or am I giving with a light heart, one that overflows with thanks to God for His goodness to me?"

If you cannot give cheerfully, if you cannot give in light-hearted love, then don't give. Close your wallet. Snap your checkbook shut. God does not need your money, and giving under the compulsion of guilt or the mistaken notion of making points with your Father will damage you spiritually.

Your Lord doesn't want to see you hurt yourself, especially not under the guise of giving Him a gift. So wait awhile. Ask Him to show you any fear, selfishness, or lovelessness that might have hardened on the walls of your heart. Then confess any sin He reveals to Him and ask Him to melt those things away.

The apostle Paul once told the believers in the city of Corinth:

> Each man should give what he has decided in his heart to give, not reluctantly or under compulsion, for God loves a cheerful giver. And God is able to make *all* grace abound to you, so that in *all* things at *all* times, having *all* that you need, you will abound in *every* good work. . . . You will be made rich in *every* way so that you can be generous on *every* occasion, and through us your generosity will result in thanksgiving to God (2 Corinthians 9:7, 8, 11; italics added).

Count the *alls* and the *everys* in Paul's words. It's quite a promise our Lord makes to us here. He leaves it up to us to decide what we want to give. Then He takes the responsibility for seeing to it that we continue to have all that we need ourselves.

The key, though, lies in the word cheerful. The New Testament Greek root is the word from which we derive the English word *hilarious.* I once attended a worship service in a congregation away from home. At a certain point in the service, the pastor told the worshipers that God would now give them a chance to give. As the ushers came forward with the offering baskets, the congregation began to applaud. Everyone, it seemed, burst into a big grin. I'm sure our Lord was smiling, too.

That offering was the most light-hearted and at the same time, the most worshipful offering I've ever seen. God gave us a chance to give. What a blessing!

• • •

I know God wants me to give with a cheerful heart. But I still want to know how much He expects from me.

If you're looking for a percentage or a dollar amount, your heart is still in the wrong place. God required 10 percent from His Old Testament people. That requirement was abolished when Jesus died. You're free from the demands of the law. You're free to decide what you want to give.

Look at it this way. When you decide on a birthday gift for someone you love very much, do you take out your calculator and figure the minimum price tag your loved one will expect in light of your current income? Probably not. Why, then, would we think that our heavenly Father wants us to treat Him that way?

Does the New Testament lay out any guidelines at all about how much to give?

In his first letter to the church in Corinth, Paul wrote about a special offering he had organized to benefit believers in Jerusalem. These saints had fallen into severe hardship, perhaps due to a famine or perhaps because they were being persecuted for their faith in Jesus. Paul laid out some guidelines for the believers in Corinth to consider as they planned their contribution:

> On the first day of every week, each one of you should set aside a sum of money in keeping with his income, saving it up, so that when I come no [additional] collections will have to be made (1 Corinthians 16:2).

Paul's refers to a special offering. Still, without violating the text, we can pull from this passage some basic principles about giving.

First of all, the amount we give should be in some measure proportional to the amount we earn, a percentage of our income. Those who earn more can afford to give more.

We can also infer from Paul's words that God wants His people to give on a regular, planned basis. Note, though, that this is for our benefit, not His. Remember, He does not need our money. But we need to remember God's goodness to us. Week by week, we need to invite God to examine our hearts. We need to ask Him for help in spotting any idols of silver or gold, wood or stone, that have lodged there. Week by week, we need to ask His help in evicting these false gods from our heart for He wants us to have the joy of giving, of honoring Him with our gifts.

How do I decide where to give? Who should get my offerings?

The first and largest portion of the money you decide to give to God belongs in your local congregation, the place where you are fed, nurtured, and encouraged in your Christian faith. The Scriptures clearly state that those who feed on God's Word should care for the physical, material, financial needs of those who shepherd them. (See 1 Corinthians 9:1–14 and 1 Timothy 5:17–18.)

Besides paying your pastor and, possibly, other staff people, your local congregation will use your offering to fund various programs that support and uplift your fellow believers and to finance the outreach efforts your Lord leads the decision-makers in your church to support.

Make no mistake, though. When you bring your offering to God's house, God wants you to give it *from* a thankful heart, not *to* a specific person or program. Remembering this distinction will protect you from thinking of your offering as a "purchase of services" agreement like the kind you might make with your local appliance dealer or computer repair shop.

Instead, God wants you to view your offering as a gift to Him, a gift that overflows in your life from the thankful heart He has first given you. Then, when your pastor or your congregation ministers to you, you can trust they do that for similar reasons; their ministry to you comes from the thankful, loving hearts God has placed within them. Your pastor and your congregation do not owe you anything in return for your regular or generous contributions, no matter how regular or how generous your giving has been.

What about giving to ministries or causes outside my local congregation?

You're free, as a manager of the resources God has given you, to do that. As you do so, though, keep these principles in mind:

- The Christian's primary responsibility is to help fellow believers, those who belong to the "household of faith" (Galatians 6:10 NASB).
- As faithful managers of God's resources, we should not give blindly to outside organizations assuming they will use our money with fiscal integrity. Even Christian organizations sometimes go astray. Check out their credentials before you decide to give to them.
- Remember that there will always be more requests than resources. If you were to spend the next few days giving away every dime you now own, you would scarcely dent

the world's great need. No matter how rich you are, you would not abolish unbelief, hunger, disease, or any other of humanity's scourges by impoverishing yourself. Use wisdom as you decide how to allocate your Father's riches.

What if I disagree with the way my congregation budgets its money?

First of all, remember once again that as you give in your local congregation, God wants you to give *from* a thankful heart, not *to* a specific program or person. In one sense, when your money leaves your hands it becomes God's responsibility. He holds the leaders of your congregation responsible for using it wisely.

This truth removes any right you think you might have to put your congregation's financial records under a microscope after each Sunday's service.

On the other hand, ministries and ministers sometimes fall into sin. If you have questions about the financial affairs of your congregation, sit down and talk with those in charge. They may have facts that you know nothing about. On the other hand, God may want to use you to confront your leaders—gently and with respect—about details they have overlooked, mistakes they have made, or even sins they have committed. In most cases, though, a simple conversation will clear up any questions you may have.

For further reading: 2 Corinthians 8 and 9

Dear Terry,

Your last letter encouraged me more than I can say! I guess I hadn't realized that God cares so much about the details of my life, even the financial details. He trusts me to manage His resources. Wow!

If I read you right, you're saying that the Lord wants to help me plan and prioritize my time and my money so that my life counts and has real meaning and also so that I enjoy what I do and enjoy the relationships He's given me—with Himself and with other people.

It sounds so idealistic! But I guess the kind of attitude and balance you're talking about don't sprout up, full-grown, overnight. I can see I have some growing to do in that area!

I need to grow in so many ways! Take worship, for instance. I find myself really puzzled—about worship services in church, I mean. Pastor Bartlett keeps talking about how important worship is. I do honestly enjoy talking with folks before and after the services. And I enjoy Sunday morning Bible class a lot, even though I sometimes feel like I don't know enough to go to Bible class.

But I just don't seem to get what I had hoped out of the service itself. I know it's an obligation I have as a Christian, at least I think so. I never have liked to sing. Maybe that's part of the problem. And I sometimes daydream my way through sermons, even though I try hard to pay attention.

Is there something wrong with me, Terry? Do you like to worship? Maybe there's a deeper question here, one like, what is worship anyway?

Thanks, Terry!

Lynn

Oh, magnify the Lord with me,
And let us exalt His name together. Psalm 34:3 (NKJV)

What about Worship?

"How do you expect a person to play Beethoven on a toy violin?" That's Schroeder's question when Charlie Brown offers to let him try out a new instrument.

Have you ever felt like that—inadequate? Maybe you've never thought of worship in quite this way before. Try this picture out now: Imagine yourself standing at the doorway of heaven's throne room. Imagine walking through that doorway and down a seemingly endless aisle. Imagine millions and millions of holy angels filling the room, all shouting praise to the Creator-King of the universe.

Now picture yourself standing in the glow of the majesty that shines from God's throne, a plastic violin in hand and smudges on your face, proposing to play a melody in praise to God.

Schroeder with a toy violin. In a sense, that's what we are as we enter God's presence to worship Him—hopelessly inadequate. Nothing we could ever do or say or sing could possibly amplify God's glory or increase His goodness. What do we have to offer the immortal, invisible, all-glorious God?

Those truths could send us slinking out the nearest side door. But wait! Don't leave just yet!

Our God has chosen us to be His very own children. He's adopted us. We're the King's kids, and we're welcome in His presence. He wants us there. He Himself has invited us. We're forgiven. We were hostages to sin and Satan, but the Father's one and only Son has paid the ransom to set us free.

In fact, knowing what Jesus has done for us makes it possible for us to praise our God in a way that even the holy angels themselves cannot. They do not know the joy of forgiveness, of rescue, of love that paid such a price to win them back. They cannot praise God from a heart touched by His forgiving grace.

But we can! Can we ever! Our sins forgiven, our guilt taken away, we're welcome in God's presence. We belong here. Our King has said so Himself.

Many people think of worship in terms of doing something for God, in terms of obligation. Nothing could be further from the truth.

The main thing in worship is not what we offer our Lord, but what He gives to us. As we participate in a worship *service*, it's God who does the serving:

- God draws us and our Christian brothers and sisters into His presence.
- God speaks to us through His Word.
- God confronts us with our sin and warns us of its dangers.
- God assures us of His forgiveness and gives us His power to overcome our sin.
- God encourages us with the Good News of His love and with His promises of strength to meet the specific challenges we face.
- God spreads the banquet table of Holy Communion and invites us to receive His forgiveness and love in tangible form.

Your Savior wants to do all these things for you—for you personally! Still, all too often God's people walk away from a worship service spiritually hungry, dry, empty. Why? And perhaps more to the point, how can you "get more out of it" when you worship?

First, ask the Holy Spirit to banish from your mind the idea that worship is a way you earn God's favor or avoid His anger. Ask the Holy Spirit to help you see worship as God's gift to you. You cannot earn that gift, but you can prepare yourself to receive it. Here's how:

- *Ask* your Lord to create in your heart a desire to experience His presence as you worship. Because God is holy and we are not, we often shy away from Him. Even without realizing it, we tend to hold ourselves back. Ask your Lord to wash away your reluctance to meet with Him.
- *Expect* your Lord to be present in a unique and powerful way as you worship Him with other believers. He's promised to do that. Jesus said, "Where two or three come together in My name, there am I with them" (Matthew 18:20).
- *Open* your heart as you enter your Lord's presence. Let Him shine His search light into all the dark corners there. Confess any sin He shows you.
- *Receive* your Lord's unconditional love and His forgiveness

for all your sins. Bask in the light of that love and forgiveness.

- *Ask* your Lord to speak to you through His Word about specific needs in your life and expect Him to do that.
- *Think* about your Lord's goodness to you and the specific ways He's blessed you, especially in the time since you last worshiped Him.
- *Remember* the power that's released when God's people pray together. Jesus has promised, "If two of you on earth agree about anything you ask for, it will be done for you by My Father in heaven" (Matthew 18:19). Think about the words of the prayers and join in those words from your heart.
- *Rejoice* that your Lord invites you to His Table and that He meets you there to forgive and strengthen you. Come to His Supper expecting Him to touch your heart and change your life.
- *Look* for ways to encourage others who worship with you as you have opportunities to greet them and talk with them.

The Creator of the universe does not need our praise. He does not need our worship. But we need to praise Him. The psalms often use the little phrase, "Oh, magnify the Lord" (e.g., Psalm 34:3 NKJV). God won't get any bigger because we praise Him. He won't grow in goodness as a result of our worship. The thought is preposterous.

But our picture of Him grows as He ministers to us in worship. He magnifies our vision of His love. He enlarges our understanding of His magnificent grace. As He does that, we grow spiritually. We grow more like Jesus. That is God's ultimate goal for us, and it's our goal, too.

• • •

What does it mean that "God is present in a unique and powerful way" when we worship? Isn't He everywhere all the time?

Yes, He is. An Old Testament prophet wrote:

"Can anyone hide in secret places so that I cannot see him?" declares the Lord. "Do not I fill heaven and earth?" declares the

Lord (Jeremiah 23:24).

On the other hand, the Lord Jesus promised His followers, "Where two or three come together in My name, there am I with them" (Matthew 18:20). As good Jews, the disciples to whom our Lord first spoke this promise already knew that God was omnipresent (present everywhere). They would have understood Jesus' words, then, to point to something else, something deeper.

The Lord would reveal Himself to His followers when they came together "in [His] name." He would pour out His love and power as they met together. They would know He was among them; they would experience His presence in a way different from that of private prayer or Bible study—important and powerful as these things are.

As we ask our Lord to prepare our hearts and lead us into worship with other believers, we experience this mystery. We will never understand it completely, at least not until we join the choirs of heaven in person. But we do get to enjoy it and grow through it even now.

I'd like to go to Bible class, but I feel that I don't know enough. What should a person know to feel comfortable?

You might be surprised to find out how many Christians feel exactly the way you do. Some of them are new believers, but some have been Christians for years and years.

Think of it this way. Suppose you wanted to learn to operate a computer. Would you feel embarrassed to show up at computer class the first day because you didn't know the difference between hardware and software? Or suppose you wanted to learn the art of Oriental cooking. Would you avoid a class offered at your local community college just because you've never seen ginger root or bok choy?

Most people enroll in a computer class or a cooking class precisely because they don't know all there is to know about computers or cooking. Believers join Bible classes because they want to learn more about God's book and especially because they want to learn to know their Lord better.

I feel frustrated in Bible class because everyone else

**seems to find their place in the Bible before I do.
How can I participate without feeling foolish?**

Sometimes Christians feel awkward in Bible class primarily because the leader scoots from one passage of Scripture to the next and then on to the third—bang, bang, bang! Students new to Bible study can find this frustrating. If others seem to find their way around from text to text with ease, you may find yourself flustered and maybe even embarrassed.

If you struggle with this, talk with your class leader in private. Explain your problem. Ask for a list of texts ahead of time, look them up, and mark them with slips of paper in your own study Bible.

Or ask your leader to think about distributing a set of identical Bibles for use in class. Then the leader can call out page numbers in addition to chapter and verse references.

Finally, you might want to index your Bible. Many Bible bookstores sell sets of small tabs you can use to mark the first page of each Bible book. If you attach a set of these to the pages of your personal study Bible, you'll likely find yourself much less frustrated in group Bible studies.

For further reading: Psalm 119:169–76 (a good prayer to pray before the worship service begins!); John 4:21–24

69

Dear Terry,

Thanks for explaining what worship can be. God's really something, isn't He? To think that He invites us—invites me—into His presence to meet with Him. To think that He wants to give Himself, more and more of Himself, to me. Wow!

Pastor Bartlett has talked with me several times in the past few months about joining here at Immanuel when the adult information class ends. After I got your letter about worship, I almost phoned him to say yes right then and there.

But I backed off again. I'm not quite sure why, except that I take my commitments seriously. Maybe too seriously; I don't know. I just don't want to say I want to belong here and then find I'm sorry later.

Maybe I'm not sure I want to be tied down. I mean, I like the people and the church well enough right now. Things are going great. But what will happen when the honeymoon ends, so to speak?

Can't I get the benefits of having a church without signing on the dotted line? Can't I just keep worshiping here and attending Bible class without all the formality of establishing an official membership? I guess I'm really asking why I should bother to belong to any specific church, or even why I should want to belong.

I know you feel strongly about this, because I've heard you talk about it before. I don't remember what you said, though. So here's your chance to explain once again. (I'll try to pay attention this time!)

Thanks one more time, Terry, for your patience and your concern. You're one special person!

Love in Jesus,

Lynn

The whole is greater than the sum of its parts.

Why Do I Need a Church?

One spring day while Jim Thorpe, the future Olympic star, was still in college, he competed in a track meet far from home. The opposing team came out to the train station to meet the team from Thorpe's school.

Imagine their surprise when only two people got off the train— Thorpe and his coach. Thorpe's opponents nearly laughed him back on the train. Who ever heard of a "track team" made up of one person?

They didn't laugh long. Thorpe won his first event, then his second, then his third. He stacked up eight victories that day, and with those eight victories enough points to win the meet—all by himself!

Despite Jim Thorpe's success, few athletes today would compete single-handedly against a whole team. Few lone rangers make it in the world of team sports. Somewhat surprisingly, though, numbers of individual Christians try to do something just like it. Believers who have left the starting blocks well and who, by God's grace, have begun a strong race of faith, sometimes manage to trip over one of Satan's favorite temptations: the illusion they can survive and even thrive with a lone-ranger faith, the illusion they do not need to commit themselves to a specific group of fellow believers, a local congregation.

New believers often snap unsuspectingly at this lure, only to find themselves yanked rudely out of the water and suffocating spiritually on the beach before they realize that Satan has managed to hook them. Needing other Christians quite literally is a matter of life and death, spiritual life and death.

The mirage of "private faith" entices some experienced believers, too. Probably all of us at one time or another find ourselves tempted to leave the oasis of Christ's church to wander off on our own in search of something cooler and sweeter, something less restrictive, more spiritually refreshing. Those who do strike out into that desert on their own and who, by God's grace, eventually make it back, tell tales of dryness and misery. They warn us, as God's Word has already warned us, that nothing lies outside the oasis our Lord has provided—nothing but danger and death.

Despite all the warnings the mirage continues to seduce so many. That alone makes it legitimate to ask this question: Why do I need a church? Why do I need to be committed to a local congregation? There's nothing wrong in asking. For one thing, knowing the answer can help inoculate us against this particular scheme of the devil. And it can provide direction as we look for a specific congregation to which we will commit ourselves.

Family

Why do I need a church? If you were to ask your Lord Jesus that question, He would probably begin by explaining that His church is now your family.

Remember that when you came to faith, you did not simply acknowledge a new set of facts about spiritual things. Rather, you entered a new relationship, in fact a whole new set of relationships. Scripture makes it clear that these relationships are family relationships. Jesus has become your brother, and because of Jesus, you can call God "Father."

You belong to the family of God, and you're not in the family by yourself. You belong to the other members of our Father's family, and we belong to you. No one lives in this family long before we notice one another's virtues and vices, wisdom and warts. For better or worse, we're all in the family together. Membership is not optional; it's simply the way things are. And it's a good thing, because we need each other.

Why do I need a church? Because I belong to God and He says I now belong to the other members of His family, too.

Feeding

Believers need the church—and, more specifically, a local congregation—because we all need to be fed spiritually. In the local congregation, believers gather week by week, month by month, year by year, decade by decade, to hear God's Word taught, preached, prayed, and sung. As we gather, our Good Shepherd takes His sheep to lush pastures.

Our Lord does not gather His family and then feed us the dried up grass of human wisdom. Our Lord does not gather His family and then expect us to gnaw on the sticks and straw of human ideas or philosophies. No. As we gather, our Lord feeds us on His Word, the Word that nourishes us and refreshes us, the Word that reminds us that we're forgiven and free! And as we hear that Word, the Holy Spirit creates strength and joy in our hearts:

> As the rain and the snow
>   come down from heaven,
> and do not return to it
>   without watering the earth
> and making it bud and flourish,
>   so that it yields seed for the sower and bread for the eater,
> so is My word that goes out from My mouth:
>   It will not return to Me empty,
> but will accomplish what I desire
>   and achieve the purpose for which I sent it.
> You will go out in joy
>   and be led forth in peace;
> the mountains and hills
>   will burst into song before you,
> and all the trees of the field
>   will clap their hands (Isaiah 55:10–12).

What is God's desire? Our joy! God's purpose? Our peace! God's method? His life-changing Word!

All by itself, that would be enough. But God wants to do even more for us! As the family meets together, our holy God welcomes us to a meal, a meal the angels must certainly envy. Can't you see your Father smile as He claps His hands in command and watches as those angels of His open the double doors of heaven's banquet hall? Can't you hear our Father's voice, inviting us to come inside, to join Him and one another in the Holy Supper He has given us through His Son?

Together with our brothers and sisters, we come to the Table our Lord spreads for us. Together, we receive His forgiveness and the strength we will need to keep on going from one day to the next in the week ahead.

We come to the Table hungry. We come thirsty. We come needing more of Jesus, more of who He is and more of what He can do in our lives. We come famished—and we leave full, satisfied. Our Father has promised that to us. His children never leave His Table hungry.

Why do I need a church? Because I need to be fed.

Fellowship

Lots of social organizations have adopted the word *fellowship*. They use it as they talk about bingo games, group picnics, or the camping trips they take together.

When the Holy Spirit uses the word *fellowship* to explain the relationships that He's created in His family, though, He means something much, much deeper and more significant.

Of course, Christian groups sometimes picnic together. Christians sometimes bowl or play softball together. Christians canoe and quilt and drink coffee together. But fellowship in the biblical sense of that word refers to a set of unique spiritual transactions that happen when God's people, people committed to Him and to one another, get together.

While we paddle our canoe downstream, while we sip our coffee as we sit across the table from a Christian brother or sister, we

- share our problems and our faith;
- encourage one another in Christ's love;
- pray for one another and assure one another of our continuing prayers for each other.

We all need this kind of encouragement from one another, no matter how mature we become in the faith. Here's what the apostle Paul wrote to the congregation in Rome:

> I long to see you so that I may impart to you some spiritual gift to make you strong—that is, that you and I may be mutually encouraged by each other's faith (Romans 1:11–12).

To the congregation in Thessalonica, he wrote:

> Encourage one another and build each other up, just as in fact you are doing (1 Thessalonians 5:11).

Because we all belong to the same family, we look out for one another:

- If a brother in the faith loses a loved one to death, we take time to listen and we do what we can in an ongoing way to comfort him in his loss.
- If a sister in the faith gets sick, we take time to pray for her,

we visit or phone her, and we ask our Lord to keep us alert
to other ways we might help.
- If a Christian brother or sister begins missing worship services and Bible classes, we pray about the situation. And we
also seek that person out to ask some gentle questions and
to give some gentle encouragement.

As the Lord gives us opportunity, we care for one another in all
kinds of practical ways. We're committed to each other—in good
times and in times of trouble. And because we're committed to each
other in Christ, we can expect others in our Christian family to
show the same commitment to us when we hurt or when we have
lost our way.

Our Lord has—in grace—made us accountable to one another
as well as to Him. We're not wandering around in the desert alone.
At least, God does not want us to be.

Fellowship. It's another reason I need a church.

Focus

The sun can blaze down on a forest day after day, but no matter
how hot the summer gets, the sun will never set a forest on fire. But
if you take a magnifying glass and focus the sun's rays through it
onto a pile of leaves or twigs . . . well, that's a different story.

Individual Christians can—and do—serve others on their own.
God can and does use the efforts of individuals to achieve meaningful results. But focus the efforts of a group of believers on a specific
need, and then stand back to watch Christ's love light up the situation! Watch it ignite enthusiasm. Watch it set hearts and lives ablaze
with passion for those who hurt. Watch it burn with the steady glow
of Christlike concern and the consistency necessary to continue
caring and working until the job is done, the need met.

When we pray and work together united in our commitment to
our Lord and to His work, He multiplies our ministry.

Each of us in the family of God has specific gifts for serving others. God has given us these gifts. When we combine them, their
impact multiplies:

Just as each of us has one body with many members, and
these members do not all have the same function, so in Christ we
who are many form one body, and each member belongs to all the
others. We have different gifts, according to the grace given us. If

75

a man's gift is prophesying, let him use it in proportion to his faith. If it is serving, let him serve; if it is teaching, let him teach; if it is encouraging, let him encourage; if it is contributing to the needs of others, let him give generously; if it is leadership, let him govern diligently; if it is showing mercy, let him do it cheerfully (Romans 12:4–8).

Why do I need a church? Because other Christians and I belong to the same family. Because I'm spiritually hungry and God feeds His people as we gather together with one another. Because I need the encouragement and accountability of committed fellowship. And because my congregation provides a focus for my service to Christ, a focus that multiplies the effectiveness of that service.

Family. Feeding. Fellowship. Focus.

What a gift God has given us in His church!

• • •

What factors should I consider as I look for a church home?

Choosing a church home is one of the most important decisions you will make as you begin your walk with Christ. Pray that your Lord will lead you to a congregation in which

- Jesus Christ, crucified and risen, is the focus of the ministry that goes on there;
- God's Word receives the highest respect and human opinions and theories are subordinated to it;
- the teaching and preaching emphasize God's grace as the only power for a changed life;
- the sacraments are presented as gifts from God, as great things God does for us rather than as great things we do for Him.

What is a "spiritual mentor"?

Although the word *mentor* does not appear in the New Testament, this concept has existed in the church since New Testament times. Jesus discipled the Twelve during the three years of His public ministry. These disciples lived, laughed, ate, and sweated with Him. They went fishing with Him. They listened to Him teach. They worshiped with Him. They watched Him minister to all kinds of people caught up in all kinds of problems. In popular terminology, Jesus mentored them.

In a similar way, Paul mentored the young pastor Timothy. In his second letter to this young man, Paul wrote about that process:

> You . . . know all about my teaching, my way of life, my purpose, faith, patience, love, endurance, persecutions, [and] sufferings (2 Timothy 3:10–11).

In his letter to another young pastor, Titus, the apostle Paul wrote:

> Teach the older women to be reverent in the way they live, . . . to teach what is good. Then they can train the younger women to love their husbands and children, to be self-controlled and pure, to be busy at home, to be kind (Titus 2:3–5).

The principle seems clear. Those whom the Holy Spirit has brought to more maturity in the faith are to mentor those who are less mature. They do this both by one-on-one teaching and by living out a godly example.

Why do I need a spiritual mentor?

In Matthew 28:19, Jesus gives His church its number one mandate: "Go and make disciples of all nations." Disciple-making has been Christ's purpose for His church from the beginning, even in Old Testament times.

We all need to be discipled because we all need to grow up, to mature in our faith. We all need to let other believers help us along the road to becoming more and more like Jesus. (See, for example, Ephesians 5:19–21 or Colossians 3:12–17.)

Discipling—mentoring—has always taken place in the church on an informal basis. Yet the process that Jesus modeled and the process Paul wrote about seem more intentional, more deliberate, than the recent practice of many congregations.

How can I find a spiritual mentor?

Talk with your pastor. Explain that you would like to spend some time one-on-one with a more mature believer who could help you grow in your discipleship. Ask your pastor to introduce you to someone who might help you better understand how *to apply the Scriptures to situations you face in daily life.*

How can I get the most out of a relationship with a spiritual mentor?

Keep in mind the key phrase *mutual agreement*. Feel free to customize any plan or process you and your discipler (mentor) come up with. Here are some guidelines you may find helpful as you begin. But be sure to modify them to meet your individual circumstances.

- Interview the discipler your pastor has suggested. Talk about what you would like that person to do for you. You may want to share this list (or even a copy of this book) with your potential mentor.
- Keep your expectations clearly in mind as you ask yourselves whether each of you is willing to set aside the time necessary to make the discipling process a meaningful one.
- When you and your mentor have reached agreement on what you expect and the time frame to which you've committed, set up a standing appointment. Think about meeting one another for breakfast or lunch once a week for a specific period of time—perhaps six weeks. Plan to spend about an hour together.
- Come prepared each time to share your questions, your struggles, and your prayer requests. Ask your Lord to give each of you the grace to be transparent—honest—with Him and with each other.
- As you meet, talk about the daily Bible reading each of you has done and about the truths about Himself God has revealed as you've studied the Scriptures during the days since you last met.
- Pray for your mentor. Ask the Holy Spirit to give that person the wisdom and insight needed to help you grow in Christ.
- As the time frame on your informal contract with one another ends, discuss the future together. If each of you agrees to extend the mentoring arrangement, set another specified time frame—say, six more weeks.

What other logistics about the mentoring process do I need to consider?

- The Holy Scriptures often warn God's people about Satan's

schemes. Knowing the devil's temptations and the tendencies of our own hearts, we can conclude that, in general, women should disciple women, and men should disciple men. Paul himself seems to set that kind of principle in the passage from Titus 2 quoted above. There may, of course, be exceptions to this; we need not set up a law that Scripture itself does not. However, exceptions need to be clearly thought out. If you think your case should be an exception, you should most certainly talk it over with your pastor before you proceed.

- Choose a meeting place comfortable for both of you, a place where you can easily see and hear one another without being overheard or interrupted too often.
- Avoid making open-ended time commitments to one another. If you want to continue the mentoring relationship, continue to set informal, short-term contracts from time to time.
- Discuss telephone logistics. When is it okay to call your mentor with a prayer request or a question? Can either or both of you talk on the phone at work? during your lunch hours? in the evening?
- Be sure you feel comfortable with each other. You're going to spend quite a lot of one of your most precious resources—your time—cultivating this relationship. If your first attempt at finding a compatible mentor seems less than successful, try again with another person. Neither person should feel forced to prolong a relationship that seems for one reason or another to be going nowhere.

For further reading: 1 Corinthians 12; Hebrews 10:23–25

Dear Terry,

After your last letter arrived, I called Pastor Bartlett. Adult information class will end in a few weeks, and I've decided to make Immanuel my official church home. You were right. God has made me a part of His family. I already belong to my brothers and sisters in Christ. And I do need the gifts He wants to give me through the people at Immanuel. It all keeps coming back to an emphasis on what God wants to do for me instead of what He demands that I do for Him, doesn't it? Amazing!

I'm glad I've decided to settle down here at Immanuel. I thought maybe I'd feel more at peace once I'd made that decision. It seems that so much of the time lately I feel so empty. I ask myself what all this is about—you know, getting out of bed every morning. Why am I doing what I'm doing? What does it all mean? I know that sounds a lot like the kind of thing a sophomore in college might ask. But I am serious. And I do need to know. I want my life to count for something. To count for Jesus. But I don't know how to do it.

I thought that once I became a Christian, this kind of question would go away. It's different now, but it's still there. It may even be stronger than it was before!

Maybe I need a different job. Maybe I need to move on. On to what, I don't really know. I wonder what the Lord might have planned for my future, and I wonder how to find out. Any suggestions?

I'd welcome your comments, but most of all I'd welcome your prayers.

Thanks, Terry!

Lynn

How Can I Make My Life Count?

It's not a new question, you know. Down through the centuries people have puzzled over the apparent meaninglessness of their lives. At one point in *Macbeth*, Shakespeare's murderous king sighs:

Life's but a walking shadow,
A poor player who struts and frets his hour
upon the stage and then is heard no more.
It is a tale told by an idiot,
full of sound and fury, signifying nothing.

The writer of the book of Ecclesiastes (probably King Solomon, the wisest person other than Jesus ever born on our planet) found much of his own life meaningless, too. He wrote:

What does a man get for all the toil and anxious striving with which he labors under the sun? All his days his work is pain and grief; even at night his mind does not rest. This, too, is meaningless (Ecclesiastes 2:22–23).

Solomon had tried it all in his search for meaning. Pleasure. Great building projects. Nearly limitless wealth. Cultural activities. Hard work. The best education money can buy.

After years of trying hard, of running hard in a mad dash after the mystery of life, he summed up his race in one word. "Meaningless," he sighed. A chasing after the wind, he sneered. (See Ecclesiastes 1–2.)

Someone supposedly once asked John D. Rockefeller, "How much money is enough?" To which the tycoon is said to have replied, "Just a little more."

Of course, both folks in that conversation were talking about dollars. But if a person expects to find meaning in anything earthly life offers human beings, the question will draw the same answer. How much pleasure, power, work, accomplishment, or education are enough?

St. Augustine, one of the early leaders of the Christian church, talked often about a "God-shaped vacuum" that lies deep within every human heart. How many toys does it take to fill that vacuum?

How much is enough?

Always a little more. An address in a little better part of town. A title with a little more prestige and a little bigger desk. A few more courses leading to a degree that will bring with it a little more respect. A little bigger boat with a little bigger motor to punch up the acceleration just a little more. A few more hours to complete the next important project with a little more flair so that the boss will admire and appreciate me just a little more.

When God brought you into a relationship with Himself through faith in Jesus, your Savior, He filled the "God-shaped vacuum" Augustine talked about. God moved into your heart and made it His home address just as surely as if you'd seen a moving truck pull into your driveway. In that sense, He's filled your heart full to overflowing.

That fullness satisfies. That fullness brings a meaning to life that elbows out the need to accumulate more and more toys, titles, and trinkets. That fullness brings satisfaction.

But like a cracked pitcher that's filled to the brim, believers tend to leak spiritually. Our sense of meaning and purpose can trickle away. When that happens, we momentarily forget God's goal for us—to make us more and more like Jesus. We momentarily forget God's purpose for us—to shine through us with all of Jesus' love and peace so that others, too, will be drawn to our Savior.

Because sin and Satan and the challenges of everyday life can suck God's people dry, Paul wrote to the believers in Ephesus, "Be filled with the Spirit" (Ephesians 5:18). The Greek of this New Testament verse could, perhaps, be better translated, "Keep on being filled with the Spirit."

How does that happen? Jesus Himself answered that question:

> Which of you fathers, if your son asks for a fish, will give him a snake instead? Or if he asks for an egg, will give him a scorpion? If you then, though you are evil, know how to give good gifts to your children, how much more will your Father in heaven give the Holy Spirit to those who ask Him!" (Luke 11:11–13).

If life seems to have lost its meaning, if you feel empty, you can ask your heavenly Father to fill you—to fill you with His Spirit. You can ask Him to help you see His goal for you and His purpose for your life with clearer eyes—His eyes. Then you need to spend some time with Him in His Word letting Him do just that.

Before you came to know Christ, you never experienced spiritual hunger. No one who is physically dead gets physically hungry or thirsty. No one who's spiritually dead gets spiritually hungry or thirsty either.

But from the time you were born again by the power of the Holy Spirit, that new life God began within you has cried out for nourishment. Those who are born again "hunger and thirst for righteousness," just as our Lord Jesus said (Matthew 5:6).

Sometimes new believers mistake spiritual hunger and thirst for the kind of empty, lonely feelings they had before they knew their Savior. Sometimes they mistake spiritual hunger for the kind of meaninglessness they put up with before their new birth. It's not the same. Not at all!

What does it mean to "hunger and thirst for righteousness"? Nothing more mysterious than to want more of Jesus, to want more Christlikeness in your life. All of the Father's kids want to be like Him. We want to be like our Father, and we want to imitate our big Brother. We know, almost as if by spiritual instinct, that that's the way our lives will count for something.

Hunger like this is a normal part of our Christian life. Babies keep on getting hungry and thirsty right on into childhood and then into adolescence. In fact, they usually get hungrier with each passing day! As the growth spurt of the teen years slows, appetite usually levels off, too.

Things work a bit differently in the life of a spiritual newborn— or they should. Our Lord wants us to grow up into mature believers who never lose our spiritual hunger. In fact, He'd love it if we came to Him with a continually voracious—and continually growing— spiritual appetite! He wants us to be continually hungry and thirsty for righteousness.

Let's be precise, though, about that righteousness. Remember that our Lord has already declared us righteous in the courtroom of heaven. Jesus' righteousness came to us as a gift from our Father the moment we came to faith in Jesus. We didn't plow and plant and later pick a crop of righteousness we had grown by our own effort. We didn't even rifle through heaven's refrigerator looking for it because we were hungry. It came to us because God is good and because we were hungry.

But now, since our Lord has already made us righteous *beings*, beings with right standing in the courtroom of heaven, we have the ability to *do* righteous things. We can grow up in righteousness. The things we *do* on the outside will parallel more and more precisely the kind of *beings* God has already made us on the inside.

The more secure we grow in our *being* righteous, the hungrier and thirstier we become for *doing* righteousness. As with everything in Christ's kingdom, though, the *being* comes before the *doing*.

From another angle, we might say that the Holy Spirit gives God's children a healthy appetite. Then our Lord satisfies our hunger by giving us more of Himself, more of His righteous outlook and character. Such a deal! Such a Savior!

• • •

How can I "raid heaven's refrigerator"? In other words, what do I do when I'm spiritually hungry?

Think of it this way. Suppose you read a brochure that advertises the best caterer in town. You've heard all your friends rave about the delicacies prepared by this particular caterer who happens to be a master chef. Imagine yourself paging through the menus in the brochure and reading about the entrees the caterer offers. Imagine your mouth starting to water.

Now imagine the caterer is your father, that you've always been the apple of his eye, and that he's urged you time and again to use his delivery service—for free! Imagine your stomach growling as you phone in an order.

When the delivery truck arrives, you wouldn't lock the front door would you? You wouldn't hide and hope that the delivery person will give up and go away, would you?

When we notice pangs of spiritual hunger churning away in our soul, we can thank God that He's created that hunger in us. Then we can ask Him to satisfy us. And we can "open the front door," so to speak. We can put ourselves in a place where we will hear His Word preached and taught. We can open our Bibles on our own and expect to hear our Lord speak to our hearts. We can seek out fellowship with other Christians, telling them of our hunger, and receive God's gifts from them. We can expect Him to nourish and strengthen us.

You see, He loves us, and He's promised to do just that.

Suppose I don't feel any special spiritual hunger. What does that mean?

When people lose their physical appetite, it's generally a signal that something is physically wrong. When Christians lose their spiritual appetite, that, too, is a danger signal to which we need to pay attention.

It may not feel particularly dangerous. In fact, you may not notice it at first. But before long, the Holy Spirit will send up all kinds of flares to warn you. Don't ignore them!

Remember that Satan prowls around like a lion looking for lunch. The world system around you wants to suck you back into the muck you've now, by God's grace, left. And the enemy the Bible calls the "old nature," that leftover tendency to rebel against God, still lives in you and will push you further and further away from the Father's love and the banquet He has prepared for you in His Word.

Unlike physical starvation, the later stages of spiritual starvation seldom involve a renewed sense of hunger. Someone who starves spiritually slips back into the numbness of spiritual death without realizing it.

What should I do if I've lost my spiritual appetite?

See a doctor. *The* doctor—your Savior. Admit your problem and ask Him to treat you.

Open your heart to His examination. Specifically, ask Him to show you if anything has gotten in the way of your relationship with Him. Ask yourself some honest questions:

- Is there some area in my life in which I'm not willing to trust God, in which I feel I must remain in control?
- Am I nursing a sinful attitude or am I involved in a sinful action, knowing full well what I'm doing, but which I've refused to give up?
- Am I harboring unforgiveness in my heart toward someone?

These three kinds of sin—lack of trust, rebellion, and unforgiveness—can have an especially disruptive effect on your spiritual growth and on your personal relationship with your Savior.

Confess whatever sins the Holy Spirit brings to your attention. Then spend some time reading and thinking about passages from Scripture that promise God's people His pardon (e.g., 1 John 1:8–9; Psalm 32; Romans 3:21–24; Romans 8:1).

Once your Doctor has cleaned out the infection, rest in His love and pay close attention to getting good spiritual nutrition. Ask the Holy Spirit to guide you to parts of His Word that will help. You may want to begin with spiritual food that is easily digested—passages that have brought you special comfort and strength in the past.

Pop a praise disc into your CD player or put a worship tape into your cassette player. Ask God to lift your heart to Himself in worship. Ask Him to help you focus on His goodness, His salvation.

Look for opportunities to spend time with other believers as soon as possible. Attend public worship and group Bible study as often as you can.

If the problem persists, don't wait. Talk to your pastor or to your spiritual mentor about it. Treat a disruption in your relationship with your Lord at least as seriously as you would treat an alarming physical symptom.

For further reading: Psalm 25; 1 Peter 2:9–12

Dear Terry,

I read a book this week that reaffirmed a lot of what you said in your last letter. It, too, talked about why everyone needs a purpose for life and said lots about living for the things that make a life worthwhile.

The author asked this question: "What three things would you like people to say about you at your funeral?" If that doesn't put everything in perspective, nothing will. I thought about it for a long time, and I came up with several answers. Most of all, I'd want those who knew me to say that I became more like Jesus every day. My life would have been worthwhile if those who know me would say that about me when I've gone on to heaven.

I'm still at sea though, when it comes to making specific plans. I think I need a job change. The 55–60 hour work-weeks are getting to me.

It's not just the long hours, though. I just don't feel fulfilled or satisfied at work, and I haven't for a long while. Some of my friends say I should be glad I've got a steady pay check. They're probably right but even so, I don't think I want to spend the rest of my life hiring and firing entry level people and supervising the high school kids who stock the shelves for me.

If I boil it all down, the question amounts to this: How can I know what the Lord has in mind for me? I keep hearing some of the Christians around me talk about "God's plan for your life." How can I find that plan—His plan—for my career, for my life?

Thanks for listening, Terry!

Love in Jesus,

Lynn

Even if you're on the right track, you'll get run over if you stand still.
Will Rogers

How Can I Find God's Will for My Life?

Whatta way to go! I traveled through the midwest one summer, following one of AAA's famous TripTiks. The map makers left nothing out—detours along the way; don't-miss scenic drives; the crossroads village in Iowa that touts itself as "the birthplace of the Republican Party." Someone else planned my trip. I clicked my seat belt in place and simply drove.

Sometimes new believers get the impression that their Lord has laid out a big, fat, heavenly AAA TripTik for each one of His children. They believe He's planned our lives down to the minutest detail. A few Christians take this view to such an extreme that they hesitate before they buy this week's ice cream, wondering whether the Lord wants them to get fudge ripple or cherry vanilla.

Christians who subscribe to the celestial TripTik theory seldom believe that God has given them access to His plan for their journey through life. No. They picture God's will as a grand mystery, a mystery He's hidden somewhere deep in an obscure corner of heaven. Each Christian, they believe, must search for the path God has planned for them and then must battle to stay on course. Once a believer jumps the track in any part of life, he or she will have to settle for less than God's best from that point on. Or so these folks believe.

Other new believers pick up a very different theory of God's will for them. They think that once they've come into God's family, their heavenly Father stands by, lurking in the shadows like some white-coated lab technician. Their Lord is always with them—He's promised that. But He's present as a clinician who could, in fact, care less whether they move to Arizona next week or whether they take job X instead of job Y.

God has given these Christians no comprehensive TripTik. Not at all. They feel as though their Lord has dropped them from a helicopter into the heart of a massive forest. They've landed without so much as a compass. Over the roar of the engine they hear their Father shout, "Do your best, kid! See you when you get home!"

As you probably sense, neither of these views reflects reality.

The Holy Scriptures talk about finding God's will for our lives in an entirely different way, a much more comforting way. As you think about God's will for your life, you need to build on three foundational principles, biblical principles:

1. Your heavenly Father does not hide His will from you. He wants you to know it—probably quite a bit more than you yourself want to know it most of the time.

The Holy Spirit once draped a painter's smock around His shoulders and created a picture of His will, His wisdom. That portrait, found in Proverbs 8, depicts God's wisdom as an enchantress. In the word-picture, wisdom stands on the hilltops, at the busiest intersections, at the hub of every marketplace. In short, wisdom invades the epicenter of human activity. Then she shouts at the top of her lungs to get people's attention, particularly the attention of God's people.

The picture's point couldn't be more clear: Our Father *wants* us to know His will; He *wants* to help us make wise decisions.

2. Your heavenly Father wants you to grow up into Christlikeness. He wants you to grow in the ability to think like Jesus thinks, to act as Jesus would act if He walked around in your socks and shoes.

Most parents decide where and when their two-year-olds will sleep. Most parents decide where and when their five-year-olds will go to school. Most parents, though, expect a 25-year-old son to decide for himself about nap time. Most parents expect a 25-year-old daughter to decide for herself which university or trade school to attend. God wants you to grow up into similar spiritual maturity.

3. Your heavenly Father cares—cares deeply—about every detail of your life. Every detail.

Lest that truth whiz right past you, remember Jesus' declaration that His Father knows at any given moment how many hairs you have on your head (Matthew 10:30).

This means that whatever concerns you concerns Him. Nothing that bothers you lies beneath His notice. When you talk to Him about your hurts, your joys, your decisions, you have His ear. You have His undivided attention. And at the same time, in a way that no human being can understand, so do each of His other children. Like the perfect Father that He is, He wants the very best for every one of us.

With one eye on these three principles, Christian writers have spilled buckets of ink over the past few decades as they have explored ways individual believers can make decisions in line with God's will. Almost all of them suggest that you run decisions, especially important decisions, through three filters. These filters grow out of the principles you just read about.

- What does God's Word say?
- What would Jesus do?
- What would I like to do? What would bring me the most peace?

What Does God's Word Say?

The earth wobbles ever so slightly as it glides through space. It wobbles just enough that a few hundred thousand years from now, Polaris will no longer be the north star. If human beings still inhabit planet earth at that time, navigators and hikers will have to find some other way to determine true north.

Someday the Great Bear will no longer prowl across the northern sky. Orion will no longer trek his way through winter's lonely nights. Even then, though, God's Word will stand firm. The winds of time will not blow our God off the course He set for Himself before time came to be. The whims of culture and custom will continue to sway in the breeze created by the passing centuries. But our God does not and will not change His mind.

As we make decisions, we can set our sites on the principles God has revealed in His Word and know that following those principles will lead us in the direction our Lord wants us to go. We can follow His written Word with even more assurance than we'd follow the North Star.

If God's Word says, "You shall not steal," then you need not bother to ask whether your Lord might wink as you finesse your way through a shady business deal.

If God's Word says, "You shall not commit adultery," then you need not lie awake nights wondering whether your Lord might want you to have sex with the person down the hall in your apartment building when her husband leaves town on that business trip next week.

If God's Word prohibits "idols of silver and gold," then you need not tie your brain up in knots thinking of reasons God's will for you might include greed, stinginess, or workaholic behavior.

What Would Jesus Do?

When the whirlwinds of living pick up the pieces of a life and toss them aloft, those pieces don't always fall to earth in neat columns. Often—perhaps most often—the decisions Christians must make involve no clear command from God.

Should I celebrate Christmas with my family even though they ridicule my Christian faith? Or should I spend Christmas Day with my friends from church?

Should I find a retirement home for my dad who has developed Alzheimer's? Or should our family find a way to care for him in our home?

Should I agree to work every other Sunday morning even though I'll miss worship services? Or should I quit my job?

Should I fire the employee whom I've been reprimanding for six months? Or should I give her one more chance to prove herself?

The Scriptures don't speak specifically to decisions like these. What then? What if you must make choices like these?

Our Lord never intended us to use the Bible as a cookbook. As you turn to Scripture for guidance, don't thumb its pages looking for a specific recipe. Don't expect to find a list of ingredients and step-by-step instructions that will guarantee your decisions will never fall flat.

As you read the Scriptures for guidance, ask most of all for grace to know your Savior better and better, to see His character more and more clearly. Then ask for the power to become more like Him. The more that happens, the more often you will do what He wants you to do. The more like Jesus you become, the more confident you can be of making a God-pleasing choice when the heat is on.

As you face choices, ask yourself what Jesus would do. What decision would best reflect His character? What could you do to model Jesus' goodness and love to everyone around you in this particular situation? Then plug into the limitless power the Holy Spirit supplies to go ahead and do just that.

What Do I Want to Do?

Does this final question sound wrong somehow? Perhaps a bit unspiritual? It shouldn't. After all, the one who created you in the first place and then went on to recreate you in the image of His Son wants you to become as fully yourself—your true, recreated self—as you can be.

Most often, especially as you grow up in the Lord, your Father will encourage you to make decisions for yourself. As you mature in Christ you can ask Him for wisdom and then act, using the common sense He's given you. You may want to use some or all of these processes:

- Brainstorm alternatives. List all of these that you can.
- Analyze the pros and cons of each alternative.
- Ask others for advice, especially other believers.
- Then move ahead, trusting God to make any necessary course corrections. Remember, it's always easier to steer a moving ship than one that lies dead in the water.
- Ask God to keep you alert to the dangers of complacency, especially when you're sure you're on the right track. No one enjoys being run over.

In Short

What does God's Word say?
What would Jesus do?
What do I want to do?

Use these three questions as you look for ways to unknot the tangled choices everyone faces in life.

• • •

Does God ever directly intervene in our lives to make sure that we don't miss what He has in mind for us?

Of course. He loves us and He takes a personal interest in the course of our individual lives. The Bible records many examples of our Lord's intervention in the lives of His saints, His believers, down through the centuries.

How does God intervene to make sure His specific will happens in the life of an individual believer?

Down through history, our Lord has shaken many creative methods out of His sleeve. Here are three examples:

- God sends His holy angels to protect His people and to warn us of danger. For instance, St. Matthew tells us about a time when an angel warned Joseph of a plot to kill the baby Jesus. In a dream, the angel ordered Joseph to escape the jurisdiction of wicked King Herod at once. Joseph awoke, got up in the middle of the night, and fled with Mary and Jesus into Egypt where they lived in safety until Herod's death (Matthew 2:13–23).

- God arranges "divine appointments" for His people. He can see to it that we meet the right person at the right time so that we can do or say what He wants done or said. For instance, the Holy Spirit sent Philip to a road that ran through the desert from Palestine to Ethiopia. There, Philip talked about Jesus with an official of the Ethiopian government. When the official came to faith, Philip baptized him. The Christian church on the continent of Africa was almost certainly born that very day (Acts 8:26–40)!

- God sets in motion other kinds of circumstances that guide His people toward the path He wants us to take—even, at times, when we rebel. For instance, when the Lord commanded the prophet Jonah to preach a message of repentance to Israel's enemies in the city of Nineveh, Jonah boarded a ship headed in the opposite direction. Had his ship come in, it would have landed thousands of miles from Nineveh, probably in the region we call Spain today. Jonah headed for the edge of the earth to avoid God's will for him. Hardly had his ship cleared the harbor when torrents of rain and gales of wind howled down on it. The sailors put up a valiant effort to save Jonah's life, but they ended up pitching God's rebellious prophet overboard. After three days of detention inside the now-famous fish, Jonah agreed with God to head for Nineveh.

Does God still intervene in human lives in these same ways today to make sure we don't miss His will for us?

Yes. But before you take out a magnifying glass and begin to search for God's fingerprints on your own life, balance these truths:

- Most often God chooses to use ordinary events to guide us. We hear a sermon. We ask our father-in-law for advice. We look at our checkbook. When we base decisions on these everyday occurrences, we're not being somehow "unspiritual." Remember, God works through ordinary people and circumstances.
- God will on occasion use the extraordinary, even the miraculous to accomplish His purpose in our lives. His power and love burn as brightly today as they did when Jonah, Joseph, and Philip walked around on earth. While miracles are the exception in Scripture, not the rule, God did undeniably choose to act in extraordinary ways at critical points in the lives of His people. Christians can in confidence count on our Lord's love and power to accomplish His purposes in our lives today, too.
- Whether God uses ordinary or extraordinary means to guide us, He always has our good at heart. He always acts to help us, not to hurt or destroy us. Watch for His goodness in your day-to-day life. As you do that, the evidences of His love will encourage you and maybe even overwhelm you.

Speaking of circumstances . . . will they always serve as a good barometer by which to gauge God's will for my life?

No. As surely as the sun rises in the east, Satan sets out each day to harass God's people. Quite often he uses circumstances to do it. Then, too, we live in a world contaminated by human sin; other people will sometimes set up circumstances designed to manipulate us or even to hurt us.

Suppose you believe God has pointed you in a certain direction. And suppose you find doors closing in your face. What then?

As a practical rule of thumb, keep looking for keys to the door you believe your Lord wants you to enter. Failing that, look for a crowbar or even a battering ram. Look for a window into the same room. Ask others to help you bash in the door or figure out a way to pick the lock.

If God has closed an option to you, you won't get through no matter how many things you try. But if Satan or other people have thrown up roadblocks to harass you, your Lord will help you find a way around them.

Surround your struggle with prayer and keep listening to counsel from experienced believers—your pastor or other brothers and sisters in the faith whose wisdom you trust.

What happens if I make a wrong decision and miss God's will for my life in a given situation?

This question should not read "if" but rather, "when." We all fail to do God's will—many times each day. That's why John Newton, slave trader turned evangelist, once wrote this:

> How sweet the name of Jesus sounds
> In a believer's ear!
> It soothes our sorrows, heals our wounds,
> And drives away all fear.

We will often fail to find or to follow God's will for our lives. But we have a Savior. In times of failure we can remember that our Father always runs to meet His repentant children. He throws His arms open wide in welcome and meets our confession with His forgiveness.

When we stumble into the ditches of life, He picks us up, dusts us off, and sets us back on our feet. He fills us with the strength we need to put one foot in front of the other. He makes it possible for us to get back on course, to get back to the joy of fulfilling His purposes for our lives. Because we miss God's will doesn't mean He will ever stop showing us His will.

Perhaps best of all, we can trust that He will use even our detours to take us little by little toward His destination for us—perfect and complete Christlikeness.

For further reading: Proverbs 8:1–21; Romans 12:1–:2

Dear Terry,

It's official. I became a card-carrying member of Immanuel last Sunday! It took awhile for you and Pastor Bartlett to convince me. But I finally gave in.

I hadn't really expected the service to be so meaningful. After all, I've been worshiping there for several months now. But judging from the sermon, Pastor Bartlett has been reading my mail—the letters from you anyway. He repeated a lot of what you've written about why Christians need to belong to a congregation and what it means to be part of a local family of believers. Are you sure you two didn't get together to collaborate?

I've now "graduated" to a home Bible study group. We meet at Lisa and Bob McClellan's house. In fact, I went last night for the first time. I enjoyed it—I really did. And I can see it's going to stretch me spiritually. That's okay because I want to keep on growing up in Jesus.

Still, I felt a little awkward. Truth be told, more than a little. The people in the group prayed at the end. Pastor Bartlett always ended our classes with a prayer, but he did the praying himself. Last night, though, practically everyone had something to say. I didn't. In fact, I'm not sure I know how.

I've been talking to God all along, asking Him to help me and such. But listening to the others in the group pray . . . well, Terry, all my prayers seem like baby prayers.

Maybe I should have asked this long before now, but what is prayer? How should I do it? What should I say? Does God really care about all the stuff we bring to Him?

Thanks, Terry, for your time. (It would really help if you could get back to me before the group meets again next week!)

In Jesus,

Lynn

What Good Does It Do to Pray?

One day, early in the fifth century, the Christian theologian Augustine is said to have found himself trying to understand a stubborn doctrinal dilemma. As afternoon became evening, he still had not been able to untangle all the knots. So, it is said, he decided to take a walk along the beach.

As he walked, he came upon a little boy. The boy had dug a hole in the sand and was running back and forth from the ocean to the hole with a cup. The boy would run to the ocean, fill his cup, run to the hole, empty the cup, and then run back to the ocean again to get more water.

The theologian watched the boy return to the ocean again and again. Finally he asked, "What are you doing, son?"

"Emptying the ocean into my hole, sir," the boy is said to have answered.

Augustine chuckled, turned, and walked back up the beach. As he went, the truth began to dawn on him. He had spent his day doing the same thing—trying to contain an infinite God in his own finite mind.

Whether the story is true or not, it underscores an important point. Human minds boggle the moment we begin to pour into them the truth about who God is and what He has done for us, especially in Jesus, our Savior.

Take prayer for instance. Why would God—the architect of the universe—listen when we talk to Him? Why would He invite us to pray and even promise to answer us? Why would He want to keep that promise?

Yet we know He invites our prayers and that He has a long history of hearing and answering His people. Even in the times when, from our human perspective, they least deserved it. And perhaps especially then.

Gimme, Gimme, Gimme!

Understanding what the Bible promises about prayer makes emptying the ocean look simple. It promises, you see, that praying puts us into partnership with God Himself. We play an important role in the family business. We report for duty in the army our Father commands. We pray the family prayer:

> Thy kingdom come.
> Thy will be done on earth
> as it is in heaven.

We pray Christ's kingdom in. We pray and receive the coming of God's good and gracious will. The working of that will and the coming of that kingdom is, was, and always will be the primary concern of our Lord Jesus.

When we pray, we stand together with the Commander of heaven's forces and with all other believers from around our planet to oppose the forces of the kingdom of darkness—sin and Satan, hell and death. We stand together against all the misery and destruction these enemies of the cross impose on people.

We pray about many different things, but all of them somehow come back to this, that Satan's wicked, hurtful schemes for people will self-destruct and that God's mercy, goodness, and care will invade every human heart and life. That's what God wants. That's God's perfect will. And He lets us participate in causing it to happen. Think of it. He lets us participate in causing it to happen!

This perspective keeps us from perpetually praying "gimme prayers." We may (and should) ask God through Christ for the things we need and want for our own body and life. But we also focus on the other parts of God's will for us and His work in the hearts and lives of others.

A-C-T-S

Christians through the years have used this acronym to help them train the cross-hairs of their prayers on the enemy. God's people have used it to help them keep their salvos on target day by day, week by week. It's not the only way to pray, of course. But the acronym can help us organize and balance our prayers so that we mount our attack on all fronts, in all the theaters of the war Christ's church fights.

A—Adoration

Awe. Reverence. Respect. Love. Adoration includes all these

100

and more. The angels in heaven express endless praise before God's throne. We, His human creatures, join them.

We adore God for who He is—for who He is to us. We praise Him for His power, His justice, and especially for His mercy and love to us in Jesus our Savior.

Many psalms model this facet of prayer. So does Isaiah as he echoes the song of God's angels:

> Holy, holy, holy is the Lord Almighty;
> The whole earth is full of His glory (Isaiah 6:3).

Adoration differs from thanksgiving in that as we praise our Lord, we focus primarily on His character, on who He is, rather than on what He has done.

Adoration slaps Satan in the face and scatters his temptations. As we remember and speak out God's goodness and power, our hearts grow bold and confident. We have a Champion. One who has never known defeat. One who will never know defeat. Awestruck, we remember His power, His majesty, His mercy. We remember— and we bow in humble worship.

C—Confession

As Isaiah caught a glimpse of God's majesty and heard the angels hymn their praise, his heart flooded with terror. "Woe to me!" he cried, "I am ruined!" (Isaiah 6:5).

At that moment, Isaiah saw his sin as he had perhaps never seen it before. He saw the midnight of his soul. He saw it up against the noonday of God's goodness. The grisly truth of his own guilt and of the penalty he deserved for his sin crashed down around him. It burned Isaiah's soul and buckled his knees.

When we begin to praise our Lord as Isaiah did, when we recall the majesty and goodness we have come to know through His holy Word, when we speak and sing of that goodness, we also find our hearts restless and uneasy. At times, we can find ourselves over-whelmed.

As we realize God's goodness, we see more fully our own lack of goodness. Like Isaiah before us, we come to see our sin in stark contrast to our God's holiness. We, too, find ourselves wanting to hide, to escape from the blinding light of that holiness.

That's one reason we confess our sins as we approach God in

prayer. Every time we pray, we march into spiritual battle. As we enter the fray, we must disarm our enemy.

If Satan would take us on a tour of his arsenal, we'd find that two of his biggest guns are named "Guilt" and "Feelings of Unworthiness." Only he and God know how many times each day our enemy aims and fires shells from those guns dead center into human souls. When those shells hit and explode, they disable us. They can ruin our effectiveness in prayer, in witness, and in ministry for hours, weeks, or even years.

The Old Testament prophet Zechariah once saw a vision in which a man named Joshua stood before the throne of God. Zechariah identifies this Joshua as Israel's high priest. In the vision, Joshua represents God's people—the ones whom God has chosen to stand before Him in a place of honor as His priests and servants.

Zechariah writes:

> [I saw] Joshua the high priest standing before the angel of the Lord, and Satan standing at his right side to accuse him. The Lord said to Satan, "The Lord rebuke you, Satan! The Lord, who has chosen Jerusalem, rebuke you! . . ."
>
> Now Joshua was dressed in filthy clothes as he stood before the angel. The angel said to those who were standing before him, "Take off his filthy clothes."
>
> Then he said to Joshua, "See, I have taken away your sin, and I will put rich garments on you."
>
> . . . So they put a clean turban on his head and clothed him, while the angel of the Lord stood by (Zechariah 3:1–5).

This vision communicates so many more truths than we can discuss here, but note several points critical to an understanding of prayer, especially the prayer of confession:

- When we walk into God's throne room to pray, Satan often slips in beside us. He stands before God to accuse us of sin before we even get a chance to open our mouths.
- Doubtless, we're guilty. Our clothes, as it were, are soiled and torn, unfit for those who propose to come as priests and servants before the great King.
- God refuses to listen to Satan's accusations. Instead of reprimanding us, He begins to rebuke Satan for us.
- God then removes the tatters of our own goodness and

drapes the holiness of Jesus Christ Himself around our shoulders. He cleanses us from head to foot and makes us fit to approach Him.

Knowing that our Father will welcome us in this way makes it possible for us to admit our failures, our sins, to Him. We approach His throne knowing that it is a place where we will find help. Confession stops Satan in his tracks.

T—Thanksgiving

Our third prayer tactic puts us on the offensive once more. We allow ourselves to think about all God has done for us, and we thank Him for it.

In commenting on the words of the Lord's Prayer "Give us this day our daily bread," Martin Luther writes:

> This petition is chiefly directed against our worst enemy, the devil. His sole intent and desire is to take from us the things that come to us from God or to interfere with their benefiting us.
>
> So he causes endless strife, murders, riots and war; also tempests and hail to destroy crops and cattle; also pollution of the atmosphere, and so on.
>
> In short, it pains him when he sees anyone receiving a bit of bread from God and eating it in peace. If it were in his power and if, next to God, our prayers did not restrain him, we would certainly not be able to keep one blade of vegetation in the field, one penny in the house, or even one hour of our life, especially if we belong to those who have God's Word and want to be Christians (Luther's Large Catechism [St. Louis: Concordia, 1978], pp. 90–91).

It pains Satan to see us receive a bit of bread from God. It pains Satan even more to know that when we do receive God's many blessings, we recognize that they come to us from our Father's kind-hearted love. It pains Satan most of all when we return to God to thank Him for all His goodness.

Prayers of thanksgiving pain Satan. They also help prevent us from worrying about where tomorrow's lunch money and next week's car payment will come from. They remind us that we're the dearly loved children of the one who rules the universe.

Prayers of thanksgiving help us keep our perspective. We can take the long view toward today's needs and problems. We have the things that really count, the things that this world's children keep on clawing and scrambling to attain. And we have more, much more, besides:

- A heart forgiven and free.
- Peace. Hope. Joy.
- Love that flows directly from God's heart into our hearts.
- Eternal relationships with our brothers and sisters in the faith.
- The assurance that physical death is a doorway through which we will enter the presence of our Savior.
- The security of knowing God has promised to draw on the treasury of heaven to meet every one of our needs.

Prayers of thanksgiving keep our hearts safe from the artery-hardening danger of self-focus and self-reliance. As we thank God, He works in us a recognition of how dependent we are on Him and of how dependable He is. He frees us to focus on the concerns and needs of others. He frees us to focus on ways He might use us to soothe those concerns and meet those needs.

Prayers of thanksgiving keep our hearts safe from the dangers of greed. We see how much God gives and, little by little, we become givers, too—just like our Father, just like our big Brother. We lose our need to accumulate things, to heap up more and more for ourselves. We begin to find joy in passing on to others some of the gifts God has given us.

Prayers of thanksgiving keep our hearts safe from the danger of discouragement. Often when troubles come, people zero in on what they lack rather than on what they have. They concentrate on the hole and ignore the doughnut, as the old saying goes. When we let God plant and cultivate a crop of thankfulness in our hearts, we can harvest a crop of peace and even joy no matter how big the hole Satan tries to punch in the center of our lives.

Does this mean we will never battle with the temptations of worry, fear, selfishness, or discouragement again? No. But it does mean that even when Satan has taken his best shot, even when he has chased us off the battlefield, we need not sit down on the side-lines.

We can come to our Commander to do some truth-telling. We can admit our sin. We can ask for His forgiveness. We can ask Him to create within us the gift of a thankful heart. He will do that, and

He will keep on doing it as often as we need it.

S—Supplication

Practically no one uses this word today. The English word comes from the same root word as *supple*—capable of being bent or folded without breaking, cracking, or creasing. In a culture that worships independence and strength, the notion of bending before God in humility to ask for help rubs many people's fur the wrong way.

As God's people, though, we know that when we bend our knees and fold our hands to pray, our Lord takes responsibility for seeing to it that the pressures and problems of life won't break us. No matter how heavy our load, our burdens will not crush us. We need not fear that we will crack or crumble. Our God will do for us what we cannot do for ourselves.

A popular bumper sticker proclaims, "Prayer changes things." And it does. But even as we proclaim it, we should hear alarm bells clanging in our ears, warning us to avoid picturing prayer as some kind of spiritual gum-ball machine. We dare not begin to believe that if we stuff three prayers into the appropriate slot, three blessings will instantly fall from heaven on us and those we love.

Alert to the danger of making prayer mechanical and magical, some Christians have fallen into the water off the other side of the dock. "Prayer changes me," their bumper stickers proclaim. And it does. But even as we proclaim it, we should hear the alarm bells clanging again. This time, they warn us against picturing prayer as some kind of psychological trick we play on ourselves to induce relaxation and to keep us from caring so much about our problems.

Prayer is not magical. It's not a means by which we twist God's arm hard enough so that He will do something for us or give something to us. But neither does prayer simply baptize our wishful thinking. As Charlie Brown once said to Linus, "Hoping to goodness is not theologically sound." At least, not in the picture of prayer the Bible paints.

Prayer does change things. Prayer also changes us. But as we pray prayers of supplication, God wants to do even more. He wants to listen to our hurts and to comfort us. He wants to hear about our joys and rejoice with us. He wants to share our concerns for ourselves and others. He wants to lift the burdens of those concerns off our shoulders and place them squarely upon His own.

We can ask our Lord for anything—anything—we need or want and know He has heard and that He will help. He will do the very best thing for us in response to our prayers. As Martin Luther once wrote:

> None can believe how powerful prayer is, and what it is able to effect, but those who have learned it by experience.
>
> It is a great matter when in extreme need, to take hold on prayer. I know, whenever I have earnestly prayed, I have been amply heard, and have obtained more than I prayed for; God, indeed, sometimes delayed, but at last He came (Luther's Table Talk [Ann Arbor: Baker, 1979], p. 201).

This brings up the topic some have called the "problem of unanswered prayer." Note what Luther says. Note it well. Most times, God gives us more and better things than those for which we have asked Him.

Some people—egged on by hell—have painted a portrait of God as a shriveled-up old Scrooge. These folks try to convince us that even as we pray, our Father clutches His wallet, afraid He might have to release some of His wealth to pacify us.

This is not the God of the Scriptures. Our God is the one who flings heaven's windows wide and pours out an ocean of blessing for His children. (See Malachi 3:10–11.) Our God is the God Paul describes in these words:

> He who did not spare His own Son, but gave Him up for us all—how will He not also, along with Him, graciously give us all things? (Romans 8:32)

If God has given up His very own Son to death on the cross for us, how can we begin to suspect that He will withhold anything else we need to make it safely through this life and into our eternal home.

If we do not receive what we have asked from God, we need to look around. Maybe He has already given us something better instead. Or maybe that "better blessing" is still on its way.

Sometimes God delays. This can happen because the Holy Spirit needs time to prepare our hearts to receive the answer He has in mind. We often think we're ready for a particular blessing before we really are. God knows when and how we will be able to receive an answer to prayer without harm to us.

Sometimes God delays because the people around us must be changed in some way first. Situations that affect the lives of our loved ones can cause us the most confusion and pain as we pray and pray and seemingly see no answer.

This chapter began with a story about St. Augustine, the great theologian. His writings have influenced God's people down through the centuries. Yet Augustine's life began in a less than promising way. Monica, Augustine's mother, prayed for his conversion for over 30 years. Meanwhile, she watched her son waste his unholy life with prostitutes.

God loved Monica. God loved Augustine. God wanted to answer this mother's prayers for her son. But in doing so, He would not break His own rules for relationship with human beings. Chief among those principles is His refusal to turn individuals into robots. God refused to violate Augustine's free will. He refused to force Augustine to love Him. He refused to force Augustine to come to faith. He would not force Augustine to give up his self-destructive behavior.

God has not changed. Even now, He will not force change on anyone. But He will turn up the heat in people's lives in response to our prayers. He will lead us to understand what love—tough love—requires of us in a given set of circumstances. He will provide the courage we need to follow through on the decisions love demands. And He will be there to wrap His arms of comfort around us if, despite all His efforts and ours, the person we love refuses to change.

Even when all evidence seems to point to the possibility that our Lord has somehow lost our request on the floor of heaven's post office, we can know that He has heard. We can know He is at work in the situations we have turned over to Him. We can know He will do His best for us. And *His* best is much, much more than good enough.

How do we know that? Because our Lord Jesus loved us enough to fight and die for us. Our Lord Jesus has won the war for us. He marched through hell 2,000 years ago to rub Satan's nose in that victory. Our Lord has limitless love and limitless power. And He has dedicated Himself from eternity to use both continually for us.

Even so, God's army on earth still breathes the smoke of battle. We still struggle through the heat and pain of the mop-up operation. Satan's retreating troops continue to take hostages. From time to time we cringe as we see the enemy's snipers claim casualties, some of them fellow warriors whom we have come to love. Nevertheless, when the smoke of battle clears, we will stand on the winning side. We will stand with Jesus, safe and free at last.

Knowing the certainty of that celebration, we continue to pray for it:

Thy kingdom come. Thy will be done on earth as it is in heaven.

• • •

How many times can I pray for the same thing?

Jesus once told His disciples, "Ask and it will be given to you; seek and you will find; knock and the door will be opened to you" (Matthew 7:7; Luke 11:9). The meaning of Christ's verbs in the original Greek of the New Testament is this:

Ask . . . and keep on asking.

Seek . . . and keep on seeking.

Knock . . . and keep on knocking.

Jesus once told a story about a widow who pestered an unjust judge and kept on pestering him until he threw up his hands in disgust and saw to it that she got justice. Even though the judge didn't care about public opinion or about his standing in God's eyes, he heard her plea and granted her request because he got tired of hearing about her problems day after day.

This story's meaning hinges on the contrast between the disgraceful attitude of the judge and the love of our heavenly Father. If even the wicked judge finally gave in to the repeated requests of the widow, won't your Father answer your repeated requests? That's the question Jesus' parable poses. And our Lord answers His own question with a resounding YES!

So if you don't see an answer right away, keep on praying. You're always welcome in your Father's throne room.

What if I have trouble addressing God as my Father?

Sometimes believers who have grown up in dysfunctional homes struggle with this. If your earthly father was abusive, if he was physically or emotionally absent, or if his relationship with you damaged you in some other way, you may find it hard to pour out your heart to your heavenly Father.

If this is the case, feel free to take your hurts and needs to your Brother—Jesus. Pray to Him, assured that He loves you and hears you.

But as you do that, ask your Lord to lead you to someone who can help you confront and overcome the emotional and spiritual damage you have suffered. Ask (and keep on asking) for the courage to work through the pain. Doing that will eventually lead you to enjoy a fuller relationship with your God. And it will almost certainly also help you to enjoy richer relationships with other people.

Isn't thinking of prayer as "spiritual warfare" a bit much? a bit exaggerated?

Scripture itself uses this word-picture. Paul writes, "Our struggle is not against flesh and blood, but against the rulers, against the authorities, against the powers of this dark world and against the spiritual forces of evil in the heavenly realms" (Ephesians 6:12).

He goes on to talk more about the battle, about Satan's tactics, and about the defensive and offensive weapons our Captain has provided for us, including prayer (vv. 13–20).

If the Holy Spirit has chosen to use battlefield images to describe our enemy and the dangers we face, we need to pay attention. It's serious business, probably more serious than most Christians think. That may be one reason we see so many casualties.

Should I pray formal or informal prayers? Is it best if I make them up as I go along? Or should I pray prayers from a prayer book?

Both. We can learn a lot about prayer by reading and praying the prayers people of faith have recorded for us. Praying formal, printed prayers can help us balance the kinds of things we say to God and the kinds of things for which we ask. We can broaden our vision for prayer as we use prayers the church has, in its wisdom, chosen to preserve for us.

On the other hand, it's dangerous to read from a prayer book while driving to work or biking home from school. As you grow in your relationship with your Lord, you will find yourself wanting to have an ongoing conversation with Him, a conversation that runs through the day. As you stand in line at a fast-food restaurant, pray. As you garden or jog, pray. As you fold the laundry, pray. Tell God what's on your heart. Thank Him. Praise Him. Ask for His guidance, strength, and help. Intercede for your family, for your pastor, for your congregation.

Phone home often—your heavenly home, that is. The long-distance rates couldn't be more reasonable. And the response you'll receive couldn't be more remarkable.

For further reading: Luke 11:1–:13; Luke 18:1–:8

Dear Terry,

You've probably guessed already that I'm still wrestling through all kinds of questions about my future. I've spent a lot of time in prayer about it, too. My question has changed, at least in part. I was asking, "How can I find God's plan for my life?" Now it's more like, "What do I want to do with the life God has given me?"

I've begun to look for a new job, and it's really odd. Now that I've made the decision to leave, I've started to wonder how the Lord Jesus might want to use me here in the meanwhile.

Take Jeff, for instance. I'm not sure I've told you about him. He's young—barely out of high school, in fact. He started stocking shelves for me a few weeks ago. But I plan to give him more responsibility as fast as he can handle it. After you work with people awhile you develop a kind of sixth sense about them. Jeff's a winner, Terry. I'm sure of it.

It's obvious, though, that he doesn't know the Lord. I had my Bible lying on one corner of my desk last week. He thumped it as he went by and said something like, "Reading some fiction, huh?" I looked up, and I knew that he knew he'd said the wrong thing. He turned crimson and stammered out an apology. Then he beat a hasty retreat to the stock room.

I felt relieved when he left. I didn't know what to say. I want to share my faith with other people, but I guess I'm not the type of person who does that kind of thing very well. It just goes to show there's a reason I'm in management, not sales. Is that wrong? I feel uneasy about it. Guilty, I guess. Help!

> *Confused,*

Lynn

Some want to live within the sound
of church or chapel bell;
I want to run a rescue shop
within a yard of hell. C. T. Studd

How Can I Share Jesus' Love with Others?

Quaint. All this talk of chapel bells and rescue shops rings with the muffled notes of another time, another place.

Christians of bygone years understood—from their hearts—the reality of hell, of heaven, of human sin, and the human need for rescue. They saw the kingdom of God at war—literally—with the forces of Satan. And they believed Jesus' promise:

> I will build My church, and the gates of hell [hades] will not overpower it (Matthew 16:18 NET).

The church marched forward at Christ's command, forward to the very gates of hell. True to His Word, the Lord Jesus flattened those gates before His army. Dozens, hundreds, thousands, millions found themselves liberated from slavery to Satan and sin. They flooded into the safety of the Savior's arms.

Quaint.

Or so most people in our culture find all this talk about spiritual warfare and angel armies. Many find it more than quaint. They might use words like *intolerant* or *dangerous*. And some inside the organizational church agree. Demons? Hell? Rescue mission? Powers of evil? Who thinks in these terms anymore?

But before we banish these ideas to the storeroom in the church basement as so many antiques left over from a more superstitious time, we need to take a closer look. We need to wake up and smell the smoke that wafts into the church building from the battlefields outside and especially that which often rises from inside. We need to listen to the roar of the spiritual battle our Lord Jesus so often warned His disciples about.

Why Would I Want to Witness?

Just as Satan would like to convince God's people that prayer involves nothing more than pious feelings and accomplishes no more than helping us adjust to the inevitable, so he would like to convince us that heaven's war with hell has ended, that peace has broken out between the kingdoms of darkness and light. Nothing would please Satan more than to convince us to ignore Christ's call to battle and to sit around the campfire instead, regaling one another with war stories from centuries gone by.

This temptation has overtaken and subdued whole battalions of believers. Our enemy did not, could not, and even now cannot persecute or propagandize the church of Jesus Christ into submission. So, like the famous fog of Carl Sandburg's Chicago, he creeps in on little cat feet. Silent. Unnoticed. Clouding our vision. Anesthetizing us to the pain of those still trapped in the horror of spiritual death.

Still, the marching orders our Lord gave His first-century church have not changed. "Go," He said, "Disciple the nations. Baptize. Teach" (paraphrased from Matthew 28:19–20). We want to share Jesus' love because He has told us to do it.

Even if we had no command to bring others into Jesus' presence and under the influence of His love, we could scarcely help doing that anyway. When we truly see how good the Good News of what He has done for us is, how can we help but do cartwheels and back flips over it?

If you are a newborn Christian, you will almost surely, over time, forget the pain of living in spiritual death. Those who have been believers from early childhood have never experienced that kind of death and can't quite understand it. The loneliness. The gnawing emptiness. The unanswered, unanswerable questions. Or the numbness that engulfs the spirit and keeps the nagging twinge of spiritual emptiness from growing into a roar of pain that demands attention.

But God's newborn children know. That's one reason the church needs new believers so much. Newborn Christians remember. They know, firsthand, the reality and relief of rescue. They know, firsthand, the pricelessness of the friendship Jesus offers. They know it, because they've lived without it.

No wonder new believers often struggle with the temptation to grab the lapels of strangers on the street to urge them to receive the great gift God offers to everyone. New believers know how important witnessing is. They feel it in their bones. That's almost certainly why the Lord Jesus urged the believers in the city of Ephesus,

"Return to your first love!" (paraphrased; see Revelation 2:4–5).

A passionate love for Jesus spills over into every part of life. In fact, the spiritual impact we have on the lives of others can grow only as the Holy Spirit works in us a deep awareness of God's love for us and a passionate commitment to Him. That kind of passion throws caution to the winds. It leaps in to love people, to love them despite the price our Lord paid for loving, despite the price that we know we too will pay.

Life on the edge. That's the life of Christian witness. The next challenge, the next adventure lies just around the corner. New opportunities pop up with each day's sunrise. New chances to be Jesus in the lives of people appear with each morning's dew. What a way to live!

Despite all this, some of God's people manage to turn witnessing into another religious have-to. They twist God's blessing into a grotesque rule. If that begins to happen in your life, take a moment. Look around. Lift your nose and sniff the air for a hint of smoldering sulphur. Chances are good you'll catch a whiff of it. Hell has been at work.

Then think about our Lord Jesus. When He lived on first-century earth, He couldn't get enough of serving people. At times, He forgot about food. He sometimes postponed sleep. Why? Because of all the chances His Father had given Him to show the Father's concern and to talk about His Father's kingdom.

Jesus saw that kingdom coming. He saw it overtaking the sadness, the tragedy, the separation, and the death that had blanketed earth's people for so many centuries under Satan's demonic rule. Jesus burst with joy in bringing the kingdom of God into people's lives. He burst with joy in assuring them that His Father would forgive, that His Father did love, that His Father would comfort, heal, and help—no matter how serious the problem or the pain people faced.

Jesus brought Good News. And He knew it.

Now Jesus has given us the chance to finish what He started. We get to be windows through which His love will shine into the darkness of people's lives. He assures us He will stay with us and that He will give us whatever we need—whatever we need—to fulfill the assignments He has made.

We don't witness to people so that we can cut more notches into the binding of our Bible.

We don't witness to people to earn special favors from God.

We don't witness to people because we have all the answers for their need. We probably don't even know all the questions.

We don't witness because we have to.

We witness because we get to. We witness because, like our Lord's apostles, we can't stop talking about the things we've seen and heard (see Acts 4:20). The Holy Spirit is teaching us how to live the way Jesus lived. The Holy Spirit is teaching us to think like Jesus, to speak like Jesus, to act like Jesus. And that, quite simply, is what a life of witness is all about.

Why Would Someone Want to Listen to My Witness?

Maybe they wouldn't. In fact, chances are good that few people will sit and listen to you talk about your Lord during the first hours or weeks of friendship with you.

Most witness—not all, but most—begins with what we do rather than with what we say. As many evangelists have so aptly pointed out, most people are loved into our Father's kingdom, not argued into it.

People around us live in our spiritual and emotional sphere of influence. They watch as our boat bobs alongside theirs. They see us ride the high tides, and they watch us set our sails as we head into storms. They see the troubles that sometimes engulf us, and they watch the ways we relax and celebrate when the storms die down and peace descends once more.

People watch all this, not from the safety of the shore, but from the vantage point of fellow sailors. The tiller has calloused their hands just as it has calloused ours. The wind has burned their face just as it has burned ours. They, like we ourselves, know what it means to bail for dear life.

We need not pretend we're never tired. We need not pretend we never get seasick. We need not pretend we always sail innocently into storms, or that monsters of our own making never rile up the water.

Even so, people around us will see a difference. They will see the peace that Jesus gives us as He forgives our failures. They will see Him calm our hearts. They will see Him calm our storms—

sometimes miraculously. And even when we must buck gale-force winds and monster waves, they will see His courage win out in the end. They will see our concern for them when they face similar storms. They will see Jesus' love in our love.

They will see these things, and they will wonder. They will wonder, and some of them will be led by God's Spirit to want what we have. When they ask us about it, that same Spirit will give us the right words. Not words of argument. Not words of arrogance. Not words that sound like a thoughtless admiral humiliating a cabin boy. Not words designed to twist logic's arm behind its back and knock it to its knees in submission.

No. Words of heartfelt thankfulness to Jesus. Words of awe at His love. Words full of joy at God's call to live such an adventure.

What Could I Say?

Those who study such things tell us that almost nine of every ten people who join a church do so because a friend or family member has invited them. Nine of every ten. Of course, not everyone who joins a church knows Jesus. But as people hear Christ-centered, Bible-based teaching, the Holy Spirit has a chance to hammer the truth home in their hearts.

If all this is so, then one way to share Jesus involves no more than a simple invitation:

> Finding Philip, [Jesus] said to him, "Follow Me."
> Philip, like Andrew and Peter, was from the town of Bethsaida. Philip found Nathanael and told him, "We have found the one Moses wrote about in the Law, and about whom the prophets also wrote—Jesus of Nazareth, the son of Joseph."
> "Nazareth! Can anything good come from there?" Nathanael asked.
> "Come and see," said Philip (John 1:43–46).

Philip knew he need not argue theology with Nathanael. Even had he wanted to do that, Philip probably didn't know how to handle his friend's objection. Could anything good come from Nazareth? Godly Jews knew the promise that the Savior would be born in Bethlehem. How then could the Lord's Promised One have grown up in Nazareth? We can almost see Philip shrug. "Come and see," he says.

Nathanael did. And soon he had become part of the solid core of Jesus' followers, one of His 12 disciples.

As we tell our friends about our Lord, we can go beyond a simple invitation. Sometimes those we know aren't interested in coming to worship with us. Sometimes they think they would feel out of place. Sometimes they've been hurt by people in other churches or even by those in leadership positions in other churches. What can you say then?

Talk about what Jesus has done for you. Talk about the changes He has made in your life, about the difference in knowing His acceptance and care for you.

If someone takes issue with what you've said, don't argue. Don't feel compelled to launch all your missiles. Don't feel obligated to take potshots across your friend's bow. You need not defend God. He's quite capable of handling that job all by Himself. Simply acknowledge the disagreement and drop the topic. Who knows? God may give you another chance later on. Or maybe He'll send someone else to your friend. The Holy Spirit is responsible for the results of our witness. We are not.

Many Christians forget that truth. When we do, it's easy to become guilt-ridden. It's easy to find ourselves agonizing over what we've said and done. We can tie ourselves up in knots as we dissect our words and the other person's response.

Don't do that to yourself. God has sent the world one Savior. You're not Him. You can't save anyone. You can't convince anyone that Jesus' claims are true. Leave the work of conversion to the Holy Spirit. Dump all your worries in His lap. That's where they belong. Relax in the truth that He's fully able to melt human hearts, even the most hardened of them. After all, He's done it for you and for me, hasn't He?

● ● ●

What is "evangelism"?

This English word comes to us almost letter for letter from the Greek of the New Testament. To *evangelize* originally meant "to bring good news," and it referred in particular to news about a victory in battle.

When the Bible uses the word *evangelism*, it means much the same thing. We evangelize when we bring to people the Good News of the victory our Lord Jesus has won for us over everything that threatens to hurt or destroy us. Jesus has declawed Satan. Jesus has pulled death's teeth. Jesus has unlocked sin's dungeon. That's good news! It's news that people around us need to hear!

What does it mean to be "gifted in evangelism"?

The Scriptures demonstrate that God gives some Christians a special power as they share the Good News of our Lord Jesus, just as He gives other Christians other spiritual gifts to use to build up the body of Christ.

I spent one afternoon a few years ago distributing tracts in a large crowd at a state fair. The Lord gave me an opportunity to talk about Him with two or three people that afternoon. I had come with a friend. She distributed tracts, too. But she talked with at least three dozen people about the Lord Jesus. Four or five of them came to faith right there on the fair grounds! She prayed with them, took their names and addresses, and made arrangements to follow up on them in the days that followed.

My friend and I both fished in the same pond. We both used the same bait. What accounts for the difference? I believe God has given my friend the gift of evangelism. He's gifted me in other ways.

How do individuals know whether or not they have the gift of evangelism?

It's simple. Try it out. Paul told Timothy, "Do the work of an evangelist" (2 Timothy 4:5). There's nothing in Paul's letter to indicate that the Holy Spirit had given Timothy the gift of evangelism. Still, Paul told him to roll up his sleeves and dig in.

Most congregations have classes that will train you in helpful methods you can use to present the Christian faith, especially to unbelievers. In a class like that, you will learn important content, along with helpful ways to present it. Sign up. Take the training. Practice what you learn.

As you do that, the zeal to witness may start to burn like fire in your soul. You may find yourself standing back in amazement as people respond to the words the Holy Spirit gives you. If that happens on a consistent basis, you may indeed have this particular gift.

Thank God for it, and use it for His glory. Remember, God never gifts His people as a reward for their goodness. He never gifts His people so they can arrogate themselves over their brothers and sisters. Rather, He gives us the gifts we need to be servants for one another (1 Corinthians 12:1–31).

If I'm not gifted in evangelism, isn't witnessing a poor use of my time?

No. If you believe in Jesus, you are His witness. It comes with the package of salvation (Acts 1:7–8). You almost certainly have contacts with people who would never open the door to a Christian evangelism team. You rub shoulders everyday with people who would never set foot inside your pastor's office. God has placed these people in your sphere of influence.

Pray that God in grace will keep your eyes, ears, and heart open to ways He might want to use you in their lives. Pray that He might make you a channel of His peace into their hearts.

For further reading: Matthew 28:16–:20; John 15:5–:27

Dear Terry,

I looked at my calendar last night, and you'll never guess what I discovered—it's been a whole year since you and the evangelism team from Immanuel came to see me. It seems like only yesterday. I'm so glad our Lord sent you to me that night!

Even in saying that, Terry, I need to level with you. I guess I thought that my problems would gradually melt away when I became a Christian. Not magically. Not overnight. But by now, it seems to me that things should have become better for me.

That just hasn't happened. In fact, some things are lots worse. For instance, I've been praying and sending out resumes, but I still haven't found a different job. And I've been so busy at work that I haven't even taken a vacation.

You remember that I've written to you about Jeff—the stock clerk who's not a believer. I'm really disappointed that he hasn't responded to any of my low-key attempts to witness. In fact, he's got some of my other people snickering about my faith. Behind my back of course, since I'm the supervisor. But one kid or another drops a little innuendo almost every day. Or they'll start to tell an off-color joke and then pretend to be too embarrassed to finish it.

The worst thing, though, is that it seems that I'm struggling with sin harder than ever before. I thought that, at least, would get easier. No way.

Have I missed something somewhere along the way, Terry? Is it supposed to be this way? Thanks, as always, for listening and for all your concern.

    In Jesus,

    Lynn

The world breaks everyone and afterward many are strong at the broken places. Ernest Hemingway

Why Didn't My Problems Disappear When I Became a Christian?

Greek mythology tells of a time when the city of Phrygia looked high and low for a king. The city's god, speaking through an oracle, told the citizens of Phrygia their new ruler would come to them riding in a wagon.

While everyone stood in the city square thinking about the prophesy, a poor countryman named Gordius chanced to ride into the square, his wife and son beside him. All Phrygia welcomed Gordius as their new ruler. Grateful, Gordius dedicated his wagon to the god whose prediction had made his new position possible. Gordius tied his wagon to the god's temple with a knot that no one could untie. Once again, the oracle spoke. This time Phrygia's god predicted that whoever should unsnarl the Gordian Knot would rule all Asia.

As you might guess, many came to Phrygia on this quest. For decades, no one succeeded. Then one day Alexander the Great swept into Phrygia on the tide of his conquests. Like those before him, Alexander could not undo the Gordian Knot.

Not to be denied lordship over the known world, however, Alexander drew his sword and sliced through the knot. Later on, when his armies marched in victory across Asia, people began to believe he had legitimately met the conditions of the oracle.

Or so the story goes.

This legend lives on, or at least the term *Gordian knot* does. It refers to an intricate problem without solution. At least not a logical one. A problem one must slice through rather than untangle.

If we think very long about our lives as Christ's people, we soon run up against mysteries that make Gordius' knot look as simple as a cat's cradle threaded together by a third grader. Why doesn't God wave His hand and dismiss all our heartache? Why doesn't God stop the injustice in our world, especially the injustice that hurts His children? Why doesn't God put an end to the temptations that trip us up with such infuriating regularity? Why won't God save us from ourselves, from our own bad decisions, our own flawed judgment?

Gordian knots, aren't they?

If theologians have picked away at the strands of these questions for thousands of years, mostly without success, who could expect new Christians to untangle them?

Whether we've known Jesus for years or simply for a few weeks, we can find our emotions tied in knots over the whys of life. And if those who led you to faith in Jesus also mistakenly misled you into believing that your new relationship with Him would dissolve all your difficulties, watch out! Your Gordian knot has been doused in gasoline, and Satan is itching to torch it.

Magical Thinking

Make no mistake. Knowing the Lord Jesus brings us blessing upon blessing, blessings no one who has known them would want to live without. The peace of forgiveness. The certainty of eternal life that transforms physical death into the foyer of heaven. The joy that the one who made the universe calls me by name, loves me with unlimited love, and for Jesus' sake, has adopted me as His heir. The list could go on and on.

Still, in all honesty, we must face the fact that our Lord is not going to speak an incantation, sprinkle fairy dust, and turn our homes into Camelot. We may continue to struggle with preexisting problems. In fact, our new faith can fan some preexisting sparks into a full-blown conflagration. If that weren't enough, our relationship with Jesus will bring us new difficulties. It's guaranteed.

Temptation

Satan doesn't need to expend kilotons of energy on those who could care less about Jesus Christ. A little supervision to make sure clients like that don't inadvertently wander across the path of a loving, enthusiastic believer. A joke or two on late-night TV designed to paint the Christian faith as ridiculous. A few "accidental" encounters with church members who have armed themselves against the world with an arrogant attitude. That's all it takes for Satan to keep most of his victims in line and swaying forward to the rhythms of the death march he has orchestrated for them.

Those who belong to Satan don't struggle with temptation. They simply give in. The book of Proverbs paints their picture. They encounter opportunities for sin wide eyed, "like an ox going to the slaughter, like a deer stepping into a noose . . . like a bird darting into a snare, little knowing it will cost . . .[their] life" (7:22–23).

Those who belong to God's family, though, present Satan with a bigger challenge, bigger by several orders of magnitude. That's why our enemy invests most of his time and energy tempting us who have sworn allegiance to the Lord Jesus.

Inflamed by Satan, your flesh will try to pull you into sin. You will struggle as you have never struggled. For instance:

- Maybe, before you had read much of the Bible, you never knew that coveting was wrong. Now that God has brought you into His family, you may find yourself turning shades of green Picasso never knew about as you visit a friend's new house, take a ride in your brother's new car, or walk through the nearest mall. Your sinful flesh and Satan have teamed up against you.
- Maybe, before you became a believer, you hadn't noticed just how shady your business ethics had become. Now, you may cringe as you look through last month's files or last year's invoices. Still, the siren sings her song of profit so sweetly that you hear it in your dreams. Your sinful flesh and Satan have teamed up against you.
- Maybe, until you came to faith in Christ, you immersed yourself ever deeper in the muck of sexual sin. Now that the Holy Spirit has awakened you to the truth, your heart may ache with the shame of it all. Even so, you may find yourself drawn even more powerfully toward pornographic magazines or videos. The urge to target that married man or woman up the street or in the shipping department down-stairs may begin to grow and grow to the point that tempta-tion seems irresistible. Your flesh and Satan are at work.

If you find yourself locked in serious battle with temptation, thank God for it. Yes, I mean just that. Thank God that He's created a new you, a you that's spiritually alive. The old you never had these problems because the old you didn't want to please God, didn't care about growing into Christlikeness.

Reframe your struggle. Let it remind you that God has accom-plished great things in your heart already, and He will finish what He has started.

Then get some help. Your Savior never intended that you slog through temptation alone. Talk with older, wiser believers. Talk to your pastor or with a spiritual mentor. Pray with these people and ask them to continue to pray for you. Saturate yourself with God's Word. Come to the Lord's Table at every opportunity. Let your Savior support and strengthen you.

Persecution

Satan's schemes include no wasted energy. His purpose? To worm his way into our hearts in such a way as to separate us from our Savior and steal God's gift of eternal life from us. Failing that, our enemy continues to work so as to render us ineffective in our service and our witness.

Besides tempting us into sin, he will see to it that we face persecution for our faith. Believers of other times, other places, met death rather than renounce their Savior:

- The Roman emperor Nero tied Christians to poles in his courtyard, covered them with pitch from head to foot, and set them on fire. Thus this crazed ruler illuminated his garden parties.
- Believers in 15th-century England were burned at the stake for daring to teach their children the Apostles' Creed and the Lord's Prayer.
- Christians in 20th-century Eastern Europe who publicly confessed their Savior lost their jobs and gave up all hope of higher education for their children.

You may never stand in a Roman coliseum awaiting the leap of a hungry lion or choose between poverty and faithfulness to your Lord. That does not mean you're exempt from ridicule. It does not mean you're safe from sarcasm. It does not mean you may never lose a job or a promotion because you belong to Jesus Christ.

Your friends may look at you and shake their heads in puzzled disgust over your new faith. Members of your family may accuse you of arrogance, of hypocrisy, of thinking you're better than they. Your boss may snort at your scruples at first and then later find reasons to lock you out of the loop when bottom-line company decisions get made.

Jesus has given us many promises. All of them prove true. Most of them bring comfort. Some of them, at first blush, do not. Our

Lord has promised us that as His people we will face opposition:

> You must be on your guard. You will be handed over to the local councils and flogged in the synagogues. On account of Me you will stand before governors and kings as witnesses to them (Mark 13:9).
>
> You will be betrayed even by parents, brothers, relatives and friends, and they will put some of you to death. All men will hate you because of Me (Luke 21:16–17).
>
> If you belonged to the world, it would love you as its own. As it is, you do not belong to the world, but I have chosen you out of the world. That is why the world hates you. Remember the words I spoke to you: "No servant is greater than his master." If they persecuted Me, they will persecute you also (John 15:19–20).
>
> In fact, a time is coming when anyone who kills you will think he is offering a service to God (John 16:2).
>
> In this world you will have trouble. But take heart! I have overcome the world (John 16:33).

When you face the kinds of opposition that have come to God's people in every generation, take heart. The Holy Spirit's work has begun to show in your life. People are seeing Jesus in you. Some will wash their hands and walk away. Some will say and do hurtful things. But others will find themselves attracted to the Savior's love.

Whatever happens, don't give up. Lean on your Savior. Talk with other believers. Share your conflicts with your pastor or your spiritual mentor. Ask your brothers and sisters in faith to pray for you. And thank God for His strength, the strength that has made your faith visible, the strength that has made the change in your life and character possible, the strength that will continue to work its transformation in your heart.

A friend once asked me, "Do they know your name in hell?" As I thought about that question and about my own weakness, the thought that Satan might see me as a serious threat scared me out of my socks.

But later, as I thought about our Lord's strength and His promise to keep me in faith, my friend's question challenged me to become all that God wants me to be. Now I ask the Holy Spirit to use me in whatever ways He can as often as He can. Without false bravado, without arrogance, with trust only in my Lord, and with great malice toward Satan and his cohorts, I pray, "Lord, make me famous all over hell." That can be your prayer, too.

Frustration

No matter how far or how fast you run, you'll never run away from yourself. Maybe you've come to the Christian faith carrying scars from childhood. Maybe you spent your early years in a family that abused alcohol or drugs. Maybe you were physically or sexually abused by a relative or family friend. Maybe your parents worked endless hours, neglecting you and your needs. Maybe you've lived the life of a drug addict, an alcoholic, or a workaholic yourself.

Like it or not, traumas like these can slow or stop a person's emotional growth. Like it or not, traumas like these can retard spiritual growth, too. They can trap us in unhealthy patterns of thought and action. They can cripple our ability to form meaningful relationships. Most times the jaws of these traps close so tightly that people caught in them cannot free themselves. They need the help of our Lord and of other people if they ever hope to see the prison doors swing open.

The day Adam and Eve fell into sin, they destroyed the possibility that any child would ever grow up in a perfect family. In a very real sense, all families are dysfunctional. We all bring sinful hearts into our relationships with one another.

Chances are 100 percent, then, that you grew up in an imperfect family. Maybe, though, your family gave you enough of the right kinds of nurture to allow you to mature and to function fairly well in adult life.

On the other hand, maybe you've experienced a great deal of trauma. Even though you want with all your heart to believe that nothing much out of the ordinary has happened to you, you still may find yourself wondering, questioning.

Why do you find it so hard to trust other people? Why does that basic attitude of mistrust sometimes spill over into your relationship with God? Why do you have a screaming need to control other people and events? Why do you find yourself trapped in one hurtful relationship after another?

Or you may find yourself shut off from your emotions, numb to what you're feeling. Maybe you're frightened because you know you are even now sliding down a slippery slope toward workaholism, totally unable to stop yourself. Maybe you fight a gnawing need to be perfect in everything you do, believing that anything less than perfection makes you worthless, unlovable.

Perhaps people have accused you of trying to manipulate them, or maybe you catch yourself doing that. Maybe you experience a yawning hole at the center of your life—a hole that nothing, not even your faith in Jesus Christ, seems to fill.

Maybe you find yourself weighed down by shame—a feeling of worthlessness no matter what God says about His forgiveness, His love for you, and your cherished position in His family.

Why? Where does all this come from?

These are core emotional issues. But they intersect with spiritual ones. They can stir up so much turbulence beneath the surface of life that only the Holy Spirit Himself can keep someone who struggles with them afloat and functioning from day to day.

Nothing from our past, of course, excuses the hurt we bring into our own lives or into the lives of others. Even as we recognize the damage we've experienced, we need to remember that our Lord holds each of us individually responsible for our decisions. We cannot shift the guilt for our sins onto our parents' shoulders. And we dare not, for our own good, psychologize it away.

But neither will we exorcise the ghosts from our past by shoving the family skeletons deeper into the closet. Those ghosts can keep us trapped, cowering in fear inside emotional walls we've constructed to protect ourselves. Until we're free to grow up emotionally, we may find ourselves stuck in spiritual immaturity as well. The two often go hand in hand.

Just as God does not zap us believers immune to temptation and persecution, neither will He grant us instant emotional maturity. Unfortunately, some new believers expect this kind of magic cure. And, sadly, some Christian leaders even teach it.

But to believe that glosses over the fact that emotional growth is a process, a process our Lord Himself created and will not circumvent. To do so would turn us into emotional automatons. When we get to heaven, we will find no emotional or spiritual robots. Our Savior Himself refused to cheat the normal processes of growth. The Scriptures tell us this about 12-year-old Jesus:

> Jesus grew wiser and taller and won the approval of God and of people (Luke 2:52 NET).

What does all this mean for us? For one thing, if we're serious about growing up spiritually, we need to make sure we trust our Lord to lead us through the process of growing up emotionally. If, knowingly or unknowingly, we've dug in our heels, we need to ask Him for the courage to stop resisting Him. We need to ask Him for the grace to work through the issues that have locked us in emotional immaturity.

Growth won't happen magically. The process won't be completed in the next 24 hours. And it most certainly will not come without pain. Growing up hurts. The results will flood your life with refreshing relief, but that relief cannot come unless you take the risks necessary to the process.

Still, your Savior is not interested in cleaning out your closet simply to see you squirm. He wants to chase away the ghosts and relieve your fear. He wants to soothe the ache in your heart and fill its emptiness. Above all, He wants to heal the hurt so that you can more fully receive His love and the love of others in His family.

Your Lord will not anesthetize you to the pain of growth. He will, though, give you the courage you need to face it. He will lead you to people who will support you and guide you through the maze. He will comfort and encourage you as you go along.

If you suspect that some of the problems, especially the relationship problems, that gang up on you have their roots in unfinished emotional business, ask for help. Ask your pastor to refer you to a self-help group or to an experienced professional counselor. Ask a Christian friend to pray with you and for you.

Above all, keep on talking to your Savior. Lean on Him for courage. And thank Him for His faithfulness, faithfulness that will not let you go, faithfulness that will see you through the dark days of pain and out into the sunshine once again.

The Worst Knot of All

God walks with His children through, not around, temptation, and He strengthens us in it. He sustains us in persecution; He doesn't always end it immediately. And He refuses to cheat us out of the chance to grow up spiritually and emotionally, painful though He knows that growth sometimes proves.

In love, our Lord uses all kinds of experiences to shape us so that we become more and more like His Son. He wants us to use the temptations, the persecution, and the growth process to practice thinking, saying, and doing what Jesus would think, say, and do in our circumstances.

But what about other problems of life, the problems that plague believers and unbelievers alike? What about those things Shakespeare once called "the slings and arrows of outrageous fortune"? Why does life seem so unfair? Why all the tragedy? Why all the pain that fills so much of so many lives? Why doesn't a loving God who has the power to destroy evil just do it?

If you've ever asked questions like that, you're in good company. Centuries ago, one of God's spokespersons, the prophet Habakkuk, stormed into the throne room of heaven to demand answers to just such questions. God answered him. The answers stunned him. They stun many of God's people today, too. Let's listen in on his conversation with our Lord.

Act 1. Habakkuk is fed up. The people around him, people who are supposed to be God's people, have created a society full of violence. Injustice has swept over the nation like a tidal wave. Political corruption has so paralyzed government that the rule of law has seemingly lost all its power. People do whatever they think they can get away with.

Habakkuk lays all this out for God, as though heaven had lost touch with events on earth. Then he asks his first set of questions, questions that sound familiar to anyone who has tried to untangle the two separate strands that together form the most complex Gordian knot of all time—the simultaneous existence of an evil world and a good God.

> How long, O Lord, must I call for help, but You do not listen?
> Or cry out to You, "Violence!" but You do not save?
> Why do You make me look at injustice? Why do You tolerate wrong? (Habakkuk 1:2–3)

Habakkuk's questions did not shock God. The Lord did not scold Habakkuk for asking or send him reeling across heaven's gold-leafed floor for his impudence. Instead, the Lord answered Habakkuk.

But before He did, He issued a warning. Habakkuk might not believe the answer. Habakkuk might stagger at what he was about to hear. And so might we.

"I will confront the violence," God said in essence. "I will punish the wicked. Here's how. I'll bring an even more wicked nation on the scene. One day soon, the soldiers of Babylon will march across your country and devastate it. You think your people are violent and unjust? Wait until you see these Babylonians!"

Habakkuk's lower jaw dropped nearly to the floor. The prophet couldn't believe his ears. When the shock had worn off, he came back with a second set of questions.

Act 2. "What, Lord?" he asked, the pitch of his voice probably ascending two or three notes up the scale. "How can You do that? You're the Holy One! You're so holy You can't stand the sight of evil! How can you use evil to accomplish Your purposes? I can't believe You would do such a thing! Why would You remain silent while the wicked simply swallow the righteous? I can't believe what I'm hearing. I can't believe You'd act like that. Why would You? How could You? I'm going to stand right here; I'm not moving an inch until I hear from You."

Quite a challenge! Yet our Lord steadfastly refuses to rebuke the angry prophet. Instead, God urges Habakkuk to listen closely to the answers he is about to receive and then to write those answers down so that God's people—then and now—can read what our Lord has to say about the whole tangled mess.

Note God doesn't even try to untangle all the knotty whys. He simply knifes right through the knotted problem of pain.

"Just because you don't see justice at the moment," our Lord says, "don't infer that it will never ever come. Wait for it. I will bring justice. I will right the wrongs, ending the pain that outrages you."

Then the Lord goes on—and this is the most important part. It's as though He puts His arm around Habakkuk's shoulder, pulls the prophet up close beside Him, and whispers the one truth that brings comfort even when we don't understand life.

"Habakkuk," God says, "remember that there's a vast difference between unbelievers and My people. Those who live apart from Me must struggle on alone in their sinful pride. But the just shall live by faith." The just shall live by faith!

Those in relationship with the Lord live in faith that what we see is not all there is. Our God has promised to bring about ultimate justice, and He always keeps His Word.

While we wait for that, we can know the peace of having Him stand beside us. We can know the peace that comes from the fact that He hates the evils we face, He hates those evils even more than we do. He stands with us to throw Satan's accusations back in his face, because God Himself has declared us just, holy, righteous. He stands with us in the trenches to cry with us, to wipe away our tears, and someday to remove all the pain and tragedy that wring those tears from our eyes in the first place. Our Lord strengthens us in the fight until we see Jesus' full victory.

The whys remain unanswered, unanswerable this side of heaven. Most times we ask why, why is not our real question anyway. The question that burns in our hearts when trouble or tragedy bring us to our knees is, rather, "Lord, I need to trust You. Can I? Can I trust You even in crisis, in pain, in grief?"

- The father and mother who stand beside the casket of their infant son ask it.
- The teenager who longs to study medicine but can't put together enough money for undergraduate study asks it.
- The widow whose lonely days follow even lonelier nights in an endless march toward meaninglessness asks it.
- The grandparents whose telephone rings with the news that their grandson has committed suicide ask it.
- Those who live trapped in unrelenting pain ask it.

"Can we trust You, God? Can we? Even now? Even in the darkness? Even when nothing makes sense and no one seems to care?"

Like Alexander slicing the knot of Gordius to win Asia, our Lord cuts through our whys to touch the core of our dilemma. He uses a sword labeled "relationship." The just shall live by faith. Habakkuk understood. It was enough. He bowed in worship.

We know about that kind of faith relationship in a deeper way than Habakkuk could have. We have heard Jesus Christ scream the scream of the damned, "Why, God? Why, My God, have You forsaken Me?" (paraphrased from Matthew 27:46). Jesus hung on the cross, alone. He hung there alone so that you and I need never face anything alone. He hung there to satisfy God's justice and to make it possible for Him to declare each of us just. Righteous. Holy. Our whys melt away in the white heat of that kind of love.

I shall know why—when Time is over—
And I have ceased to wonder why—
Christ will explain each separate anguish
In the fair schoolroom of the sky.

Emily Dickinson got it right as she penned that poem. When time is over, we shall cease to wonder why. The whys will die away, replaced by the warmth of our Father's embrace.

• • •

Won't the struggle with sin get easier as I mature in my faith?

As you grow up spiritually, you will know your Lord and His Word better. You will have quicker, easier access to Scripture verses that will fit specific situations or temptations. The Holy Spirit will have more to work with as He brings to your mind specific portions of God's Word to help you through times of temptation.

Still, you will go on battling sin until Jesus comes to take you home. Think of an army advancing on the enemy. When they take one hill, they advance to the next. As God gives you victory in one area, He will bring other sinful attitudes or actions to your attention. That will often be His cue to you that He would like to help you address those things next.

Your enemies—Satan, the world system, and your own sinful flesh—will cling to you, tooth and claw, to keep you from making progress toward Christlikeness. You know that the struggle will, of course, end in victory, but on this side of heaven it will continue. (You can read about St. Paul's struggle recorded in Romans 7.)

How should I respond if people around me ridicule my faith?

First of all, don't isolate yourself from other, more mature believers. When faith is under attack, you need support.

Second, spend time in prayer—alone and with others. Pray for those responsible for the ridicule. Jesus urged His disciples to pray for their enemies. Ask God to forgive these people and to bring them to faith. Ask that He strengthen you and that He send someone to these people to share Jesus' love with them.

Third, be open to the possibility that your Lord might want to send you! Remember, most effective witnessing begins with loving actions, not words. Look for opportunities to show love.

Finally, leave the outcome of your situation in God's hands. He is ready to bless you in it and bring you through it.

What should I do if I find myself doubting God's goodness or even His existence?

Talk with Him about it. Talk with His people about it. Don't isolate yourself with your doubt. Keep on reading the Scriptures, even if they seem as dry as sawdust. They have power, the power of salvation, whether we feel that power at any given moment or not.

Someone has told the story about a pastor who visited a colleague in a neighboring church. He confided to his friend that he found himself struggling with doubt. His friend looked at him for a moment. Then he said, "I don't want to hear about your doubts. Tell me about your sins." The pastor paused, then confessed. He left assured of God's forgiveness and having forgotten his doubt.

Not all doubt is rooted in unconfessed sin, but many seeds of doubt do germinate there. If you find yourself troubled by nagging questions about God's goodness, ask the Holy Spirit to show you the sins you may have ferreted away in the dark corners of your heart. Confess the wrongs He reveals to you. Remember God's promise to forgive you. Then go back to the Word, refreshed and renewed in your relationship with your heavenly Father.

For further reading: Romans 8:31–39; Revelation 21

Dear Terry,

It helped me a lot to think through exactly what God has promised us and what He has not. I guess somewhere I had picked up the idea that my Christian faith would make life easier. And it does. But in some ways it's made it harder, too. I'm glad to know I'm not unique in that.

One thing that's bothered me a lot lately is that the other Christians around me seem so mature, so much more like Jesus than I am. They know so much about the Bible. They pray so much more than I do. It seems God answers their prayers more often than He does mine. Someone says or does something to hurt them, and they just shrug it off. I, on the other hand, catch myself plotting exquisite forms of revenge when I'm offended by someone.

Will I ever grow up, Terry? Why aren't I more like you, more like Jesus, already? Why is it taking so long?

Thanks, as always, for your help, and for taking time to answer me.

In Jesus,

Lynn

You need make no effort to grow. But let your efforts instead be concentrated on this, that you abide in the Vine. Hannah Whitehall Smith

Why Don't I See More Growth?

I once lived in a house built on a hill—low, but steep. Steep enough that it could probably pass itself off as a cliff anyplace but Colorado. For years my nieces and nephews enjoyed cutting the bottom from a cardboard carton and sliding down the hill head first. Summer or winter, the slope begged for a sled.

What's a boon for sleds, though, leaves something to be desired for lawn mowers. I approached lawn chores with caution each week my first summer there, but my confidence grew as the months passed.

After awhile, I even began to notice my surroundings as I worked. For instance, I noticed that every time I plugged in my electric mower, its sewing-machine-like purr seemed to attract the neighbor's children. They would pop out of their house directly across the street to sit on their front steps. A front row seat.

By mid-September, this had happened so many times that one afternoon I flipped the mower switch off and went over to ask the children about their fascination with my work.

"We're waiting," said the little girl.

"The guy who used to live there," said her brother, "fell down the hill three times."

"We're waiting," repeated the girl.

"To see when you'll fall, too," finished her brother.

Even as I hrumpfed and turned back to my lawn, I had to snicker. It must have been quite a sight. Lawn mower flying off in one direction. Sweaty home-owner flying off in the other. Expletives and flapdoodle. And two small children giggling with a glee that Larry, Moe, and Curly could only envy.

There's something about the old banana peel routine. And not just for kids, either. If you doubt it, think about the fascination people find in seeing those in Christian ministry slip and fall. If you've come to the Christian faith as an adult, the people who knew you in your former life are probably watching you with as much fascination as my young friends watched me. They will wait. They will watch for the inevitable fall.

Once Too Often

Everyone in North America by now has seen this bumper sticker: "Christians aren't perfect, just forgiven." Regardless of the fact that this slogan quite correctly captures the heart of the Christian faith, many still expect perfection from Christians. They ridicule or condemn any of Christ's people who fail to live up to that standard.

Maybe their reaction grows out of a need to excuse their own unbelief. ("See! I knew there was less to this Jesus stuff than meets the eye!") Maybe it grows out of a need to excuse personal wrongdoing. ("See! Jane and Joe do it, too, and they call themselves Christians!") Maybe it grows out of a need to reason their way out of being connected with the family of God. ("See! That's how hypocritical church people are! I can be a better Christian at the lake this weekend.")

None of this explains, though, the tendency in some believers' own hearts to condemn themselves when they fall. Many of us have raised this self-condemnation to a fine art. Have you ever caught yourself nursing thoughts like these:

- "There I go again. How many times will the Lord forgive me if I keep repeating this same sin?"
- "How long will this growing up process take, anyway? Why aren't I seeing more progress?"
- "Why aren't I more like (fill in the blank)? He/she never has to struggle like this."
- "When will I ever get over this (name the sin)? I'm trying so hard, but I just keep on failing."

All these statements betray thoughts focused in the wrong direction. All focus on people—on self or others—rather than on the Lord Jesus.

Late one afternoon, a five-year-old decided to climb an oak tree. Up he scrambled, branch by leafy branch. Almost at the top, he turned around and looked to see how far he'd come. Panic! He grabbed the nearest limb and hugged it for dear life. Paralyzed with fear, he couldn't see any way to go back down the way he'd come up. To climb higher would only make his predicament worse. For the next 30 minutes he sat still, whimpering.

That's how the fire fighters found him as their truck screamed to a halt beneath his tree. As the boy's rescuer reached the five-year-old, she prepared him for the descent. "Don't look down," she ordered. "Look at me. Just keep looking at me."

Focused on the fire fighter's face, the boy relaxed. The roar of panic that had filled his ears died to a whisper. After that, the rescue took only minutes.

When we find ourselves up the tree of failure, when we find ourselves stuck in a familiar loop—of greed, of worry, of bitterness, of dishonesty, of whatever—we won't escape by focusing on ourselves or on others. We must instead focus on Jesus, our only hope of rescue:

> Let us run with perseverance the race marked out for us. Let us fix our eyes on Jesus, the author and perfecter of our faith, who for the joy set before Him endured the cross, despising its shame, and sat down at the right hand of the throne of God. Consider Him who endured such opposition from sinful men, so that you will not grow weary and lose heart (Hebrews 12:1–3; emphasis added).

If we look anywhere else, if we look to anyone else, we run the risk of growing weary, of losing heart. When we focus on other people, we will always spy someone who lives a less godly life than we live. At least, outwardly so. If we fix our focus on people like that, Satan will snare us in the net of spiritual pride. With the Pharisee in Jesus' parable, we will congratulate ourselves before our Lord:

> God, I thank You that I am not like other men—robbers, evildoers, adulterers—or even like this tax collector (Luke 18:11).

When we fix our focus on other people, we will always also spy those who live more godly lives than we. At least, outwardly so. If we rivet our attention on people like that, Satan will snare us in the net of discouragement. We will convince ourselves that we don't measure up and that we never will. A two-word question lies at the end of that road—"Why try?" We will give up.

The apostle Paul saw the dangers lying along the path of comparisons. He wrote:

> We do not dare to classify or compare ourselves with some who commend themselves. When they measure themselves by themselves and compare themselves with themselves, they are not wise (2 Corinthians 10:12).

We dare not compare ourselves with others, any more than the apostle's readers in Corinth. It's not wise. We know that God does not hold us to a standard derived from the lives of other people, be they spiritual giants or spiritual dwarfs. He measures us against the standard of perfection—our Lord Jesus Christ.

If we must make comparisons, we must do so the only wise way. We need to stack our lives up against the life of our Savior. "I'll never measure up to that!" you say? On the contrary, God has seen to it that you already have. Remember our friend Habakkuk? Remember his words "The just will live by faith" (2:4)? Your Lord has already declared you just, righteous, holy. He says you measure up to Jesus. That's how He regards you.

Why bring up those objective facts here? Because those facts carry in them the seeds of the power you need to live up to the right standing with God you've received. To the extent the Spirit of God can convince you that He's made you holy, to that extent you will walk in holy living. As someone once said, holiness is not the way to Christ; Christ is the way to holiness.

Pix, Pix, Pick Up Stix

We don't always see nearly as much of that holiness in ourselves as we would like. When we look around at the debris we've created by our unholiness, we often resolve to try harder. "Screw your courage to the sticking place," Lady Macbeth told her hapless husband, "and we won't fail." No matter how reasonable that advice sounds, courage can't transform the pieces of a broken life into something that works.

When we fail, our best course lies along the road toward surrender. Listen to Jesus:

> I am the vine; you are the branches. If a man remains in Me and I in him, he will bear much fruit; apart from Me, you can do nothing (John 15:5; emphasis added).

Radical. Radical in the sense that it slashes to the root of the problem. Without Jesus, we can do . . . (*what* did He say?) nothing. Not some things. Not the easy things. Nothing. Period. If we want fruit in our lives, if we want our lives to count for Christ, then He must grow that fruit.

We can admit our helplessness. We can admit that apart from

140

Him we have no more power in spiritual matters than a dried up stick. Then we can ask Him to prune away the dead wood and to make our lives productive, fruitful, for Him.

That kind of surrender implies that we give up dictating to the Vine which fruit we want to see next. It implies that we let the Gardener decide which fruit to cultivate now.

It may help to leave the imagery of harvest for a moment and turn instead to a game you may have played in childhood—Pick Up Stix.

Remember how you held the sticks in a bundle about a foot off the floor and dropped them? Then the players would set about collecting the sticks from the pile one by one. The idea was to do this, moving only one stick at a time. If any other stick shifted, even slightly, play passed on to the next person.

Most sets of Pick Up Stix had one unique stick. Maybe the one in your game was clear or red or black. Regardless, it was unique. That stick counted for much more than any other single stick. Collecting ordinary sticks might earn two points per stick. Winning the unique stick could mean winning the game because the player who finessed it from the pile might earn 10 or even 20 points.

Sometimes we recognize the ugliness of a specific habit-sin rotting away in a dank corner of our life. Our first impulse is probably to tug away at Sin X until we loosen its roots and can pull it out for good.

All the while, we may hear the still, small voice of the Holy Spirit telling us that He wants to work on Sin Y right now instead. Maybe until Sin Y comes loose, Sin X will remain in place. If we foolishly insist on trying hard to chase Sin X from our lives, we will accomplish nothing and we will wear ourselves out by trying.

Not so long ago, I struggled with a serious inclination to gossip. It got to a point that it seemed to me that my every conversation centered on the newest negative tidbit I had picked up. For weeks on end, I anguished over this sin, confessing it night after night before I went to sleep, only to find myself enmeshed in the same thing before eight a.m. the next morning.

One Sunday I found myself sitting in a worship service in which the pastor announced the topic of that day's sermon—bitterness. I sat back in the pew and yawned. I had no problem with that particular sin.

Wrong. The pastor had uttered no more than two sentences before the truth came crashing down around my ears. In a flash of insight that could have come only from the Holy Ghost, I saw my sin for what it truly was. I gossiped only about people who had hurt me in some way. I would never have entertained the thought of taking physical revenge; that wouldn't have been "Christian." Instead, I set about shredding their good names, ruining their reputations.

That morning I confessed the unforgiveness and the bitterness that I had allowed to grow up in my heart. Gossip has not totally disappeared from my life, but that Sunday morning it ceased dominating my conversations. Even now when I catch myself gossiping, I ask God to help me see whether or not I'm holding some kind of grudge against the person I've defamed.

Sin Y needed to be taken off the pile before the Holy Spirit could remove Sin X. If you're fixated with a Sin X of your own, back off. Let God decide the sequence in which He will bring more and more Christlikeness into your life. That doesn't mean that we wink at sin. It does mean, though, that we trust Him to chip away at the hard spots in our hearts while we concentrate on doing what little we can do—focusing on Jesus and confessing our sins as He brings them to our attention.

Forgiving Yourself

A wise friend once told me, "God forgave you a long time ago. When are you going to forgive yourself?"

Because we live inside our skin, we sometimes have trouble separating who we are from what we do. Concentrating on our failures, refusing to extend the same kind of grace to ourselves that God has already extended to us in Christ, can keep us locked in the very patterns of thinking and acting that we hate so much.

God has a better way for us to view ourselves. Paul explained it to the Christians at Philippi:

> I consider everything a loss compared to the surpassing greatness of knowing Christ Jesus my Lord, for whose sake I have lost all things. I consider them rubbish, that I may gain Christ and be found in Him, not having a righteousness of my own that comes from the law, but that which is through faith in Christ—the righteousness that comes from God and is by faith. I want to know

Christ and the power of His resurrection and the fellowship of sharing in His sufferings, becoming like Him in His death, and so, somehow, to attain to the resurrection from the dead.

Not that I have already obtained all this, or have already been made perfect, but I press on to take hold of that for which Christ Jesus took hold of me. Brothers, I do not consider myself yet to have taken hold of it. But one thing I do: Forgetting what is behind and straining toward what is ahead, I press on toward the goal to win the prize for which God has called me heavenward in Christ Jesus.

All of us who are mature should take such a view of things (Philippians 3:8–15).

Want to grow up? Want to live a more and more mature Christian life? Stop believing you'll never drop the baton. Stop believing Satan's lie that God loves only those who do everything with perfection. Stop looking around the track to find someone who runs the race half as fast or twice as fast as you.

Instead, press on. Grip the baton and focus on Jesus. Focus on the prize He's won for you. Strain toward what lies ahead—more and more Christlikeness in your character. Listen as your Lord cheers you on. Remember, He's running beside you. You can't lose.

For further reading: Psalm 32; John 15:1–11

Index